CULTURES OF THE WORLD
Yemen

Anna Hestler and Jo-Ann Spilling

Marshall Cavendish
Benchmark
New York

PICTURE CREDITS

Cover: © Geopress / Getty Images

A.N.A. Press Agency: 68, 88 • alt.type/Reuters: 57, 59, 73, 107, 112, 113 • Art Directors and Trip: 69, 91 •
Bes Stock: 21, 22, 24, 25, 29, 30, 36, 63, 64, 86, 92, 105, 108, 111, 115, 125, 131 • Corbis Inc.: 8, 13, 31, 35,
79, 101, 117, 123 • Getty Images: 26, 28, 32, 34, 37, 39, 46, 48, 97, 99, 120 • HBL Network Photo Agency: 87
• Hutchison Library: 67, 78, 96 • John R. Jones: 94, 103, 127 • Lonely Planet Images: 9, 23, 41, 47, 51, 118 •
North Wind Pictures Archives: 20, 66 • Photolibrary: 1, 3, 5, 6, 7, 10, 11, 14, 15, 16, 17, 18, 19, 40, 42, 43, 44,
45, 50, 52, 53, 54, 55, 58, 60, 62, 65, 70, 71, 72, 74, 75, 76, 80, 81, 82, 84, 89, 90, 93, 95, 98, 100, 102, 104, 106,
110, 114, 116, 122, 124, 129, 130

PRECEDING PAGE

A woman walking in the old city of Sana'a in Yemen.

Publisher (U.S.): Michelle Bisson
Editors: Deborah Grahame, Mindy Pang
Copyreader: Sherry Chiger
Designers: Nancy Sabato, Bernard Go Kwang Meng
Cover picture researcher: Connie Gardner
Picture researcher: Thomas Khoo

Marshall Cavendish Benchmark
99 White Plains Road
Tarrytown, NY 10591
Website: www.marshallcavendish.us

© Times Media Private Limited 1999
© Marshall Cavendish International (Asia) Private Limited 2010
® "Cultures of the World" is a registered trademark of Times Publishing Limited.

Originated and designed by Times Media Private Limited
An imprint of Marshall Cavendish International (Asia) Private Limited
A member of Times Publishing Limited

Marshall Cavendish is a trademark of Times Publishing Limited.

Library of Congress Cataloging-in-Publication Data
Hestler, Anna.
    Yemen / by Anna Hestler and Jo-Ann Spilling. -- 2nd ed.
        p. cm. -- (Cultures of the world)
    Includes bibliographical references and index.
    Summary: "Provides comprehensive information on the geography, history,
        wildlife, governmental structure, economy, cultural diversity, peoples,
        religion, and culture of Yemen"--Provided by publisher.
    ISBN 978-0-7614-4850-1
    1. Yemen (Republic)--Juvenile literature. I. Spilling, Jo-Ann. II. Title.
    DS247.Y48H46 2010
    953.3--dc22   2009021200

Printed in China
7 6 5 4 3 2 1

CONTENTS

INTRODUCTION

VISITORS TO YEMEN ARE STRUCK by its beauty and its distinctiveness from the rest of the Arabian Peninsula. It has a diverse landscape comprising coasts, deserts, mountains, rocky plains, and green valleys. Known in ancient times as Sheba, Yemen was the fabled land of the queen of Sheba, an ancient kingdom that flourished on the fringes of the desert—affluent and powerful, situated on the all-important spice route from east to west. Civilizations thousands of years old left remnants of impressive structures as a testimony to their genius. Architectural wonders can still be found today in Yemen's capital city of Sana'a. Some ancient traditions still survive in spite of Yemen's modern developments. Although the younger generation are exposed to foreign culture through television, the Internet, and other media, many are happy to follow long-established, age-old customs. Traditional social values and family life remain intact in Yemen. Many women wear veils, some farmers still use traditional agricultural methods, and tribesmen wear handcrafted curved silver daggers. Although many aspects of modern life are moving into this medieval land, the unique Yemeni identity remains alive and well.

GEOGRAPHY

The Heiz Yazid, Doan Valley with its terraced fields and village.

CHAPTER 1

YEMEN'S ARABIC NAME, AL-YAMAN, means "southward (of Mecca)." Yemen lies on the southwestern tip of the Arabian Peninsula. Its neighboring countries are Saudi Arabia in the north and Oman in the northeast.

The southern shores meet the waters of the Gulf of Aden, a point of access to the Arabian Sea and the Indian Ocean. To the west, Yemen commands the straits of Bab al-Mandab (Gate of Lament), which is the narrow gateway to the Red Sea, the port of Jiddah in Saudi Arabia, and the Suez Canal. Across the straits are the African countries of Eritrea and Djibouti.

The desert of Ramlat al-Sab'Atayn in Yemen.

Yemen is about 203,850 square miles (527,970 square km) in area, more than twice the size of Wyoming. Yemen's territory includes some islands. Socotra in the Arabian Sea, about 621 miles (1,000 km) east of Aden, is the largest, while Kamaran and the Hanish Islands in the Red Sea and Perim Island in Bab al-Mandab are slightly smaller.

LANDSCAPE

People often think of Yemen as yet another country in the Arabian Peninsula dominated by desert. However, in addition to the rich sands of the great Arabian Desert, the Yemeni landscape has remarkable features unusual for the Arabian Peninsula: beautiful coasts and sculpted

The Red Sea, as seen from Kamaran Island.

peaks punctuated by valleys. There are no lakes or rivers, but dry riverbeds called wadis fill with seasonal rains. These topographical differences have unquestionably contributed to regional variations in culture that have evolved over thousands of years.

Yemen can be divided into four regions: the coast or the Tihama, the mountains, the Eastern Plateau and the desert, and the islands.

THE TIHAMA The Tihama, which means "Hot Earth," is a flat, narrow plain running parallel to the Red Sea. Across the water lies the East African shore, only 20 miles (32 km) away. Not surprisingly, as a result of the cultural exchanges between the people of the Tihama and their African neighbors, combined with the fact that they share a common climate and environment, some similarities appear, such as the reed huts that can be found in both areas. The sandy plain of the Tihama is 19 to 37 miles (30 to 60 km) wide. Irrigation has made parts of the plain fertile. The plain ends at rocky cliffs that are the edges of the Western Highlands. Over time, erosion of these cliffs has resulted in the formation of deep wadis. The southern coastal plain is dotted with volcanic rocks and is the site of the important port of Aden. Over hundreds of years, Aden has acted as a doorway for trade and foreign influences.

The view from the summit of the Arabian Peninsula's highest peak, Jabal al-Nabi Shu'ayb, in Yemen.

THE MOUNTAINS Mountain chains known as the Western and Central Highlands form the backbone of the country. Geologically the Arabian Peninsula was once part of the African continent. Millions of years ago a rift between the two created the Western Highlands. These mountains are made of lava and have stunning peaks that tower an average of 9,843 feet (3,000 m) above sea level. Yemen's highest peak, Jabal al-Nabi Shu'ayb, at 12,336 feet (3,760 m), is also the tallest peak of the Arabian Peninsula. Highland people living in thousands of villages perched on these craggy peaks have historically been more isolated and more cut off from outside influences than people living along the coasts. The peaks of the Central Highlands are lower at an average height of 3,281 feet (1,000 m).

Cradled within the mountainous regions lie the country's fertile plateaus that are the site of most of Yemen's urban centers, including the capital city, Sana'a.

Acacia trees dot the Rub al-Khali, or Empty Quarter, that makes up almost half of Yemen.

THE EASTERN PLATEAU AND THE DESERT The Eastern Plateau gradually merges with the vast sands of the Arabian Desert. The Rub al-Khali, which means "Empty Quarter," lies between Sana'a and Saudi Arabia.

There is little or no permanent settlement in the desert, but it is the home of nomadic herders known in Arabic as *bedu* (BEH-doo), or the bedouin, who roam across the desert in search of grazing land for their cattle.

Between the desolate hills of the Eastern Plateau and the desert, and running along the southern coastline, lies the Wadi Hadramawt, a place well known for growing dates. Located on a limestone plateau, it is just high enough to catch sufficient rain to cultivate crops. This wadi is one of the few areas in eastern Yemen fertile enough for cultivation

THE ISLANDS Yemen has about 112 islands, including Socotra, Kamaran, Perim, and the Hanish Islands. Each island has distinct climatic, geographic, and environmental characteristics. Their geographic isolation from the mainland has enabled them to develop unique cultural traditions.

The largest of the islands is Socotra, whose inhabitants are primarily Muslims of Arab, Somali, and South Asian origins. They speak Soqotri, a Semitic language. The population is estimated at 70,000, with the majority of the people concentrated in the capital town of Hadibo and the western town of Qalansiya.

SOCOTRA

Socotra, which means "Island of Bliss," is the most famous of Yemen's islands. Mountainous and semiarid, it has an area of 1,409 square miles (3,650 square km). Every year for at least four months, the people on Socotra are isolated from the outside world because monsoon winds make it difficult for planes or boats to reach them. During this period, the islanders are self-sufficient. The island's economy is based on fishing and harvesting myrrh and aloe vera leaves.

Socotra is a botanist's dream because it has numerous rare plants, but many of them are threatened with extinction due to overgrazing. Some of them are renowned for their medicinal value, including the famous Dragon's Blood Tree (Dracaena cinnabari), which is used in Asian medicine to cure eye and skin diseases. In the past the Chinese also used it for dyes and cabinet lacquers, and the medieval European scribes used it to make ink.

Due to the monsoon rains that occur from June to September, the islands have traditionally been isolated from the mainland. However, accessibility has improved since the opening of an airport in Socotra in July 1999.

Many people who live on the islands work in the fishing, livestock, and date-cultivation industries. Tourism has also become a popular way of making a living in recent years. The Yemeni government has been trying to attract investments to build up the tourism sector on many of the Yemeni islands.

CLIMATE

As the most arable spot in the Arabian Peninsula, Yemen is often called "the green land of Arabia." After the rainy season, parts of Yemen look as though they are covered with a lush green carpet. The temperature varies with topography and elevation, but it is Yemen's mountains and location at the edge of the tropics that largely determine its climate.

Agriculture in Yemen depends on moist winds known as monsoons. When the monsoon winds blow from the south and southwest, the mountains trap the limited rainfall. During the rainy season, from April/May to July/August, the rains are very irregular, usually appearing as short, localized downpours. Torrential rains can wipe out a road in one village, while a neighboring village remains dry. The Wadi Hadramawt gets a sprinkling of rain, but the summer monsoons rarely reach the Empty Quarter. Sometimes this area receives little or no rain for years, making it virtually impossible to cultivate crops there. Such unpredictable rains have challenged generations of farmers to build elaborate terraces and irrigation systems to trap the scanty rainfall.

Yemen's regional climate varies considerably. The Western and Central Highlands are drier and cooler than the rest of the country. It has been said that the air in those regions is "as temperate and sweet as the fresh spring." The winter season, from December to February, can get chilly, though, with temperatures sometimes dropping below freezing. Cozy sheepskin jackets keep the highlanders warm during the winter.

Along the Red Sea and the southern coast, the climate is hot and humid. Temperatures can rise to 104°F (40°C) during June and July. To stay cool, people along the coast wear very loose clothes.

The desert and the Eastern Plateau are blisteringly hot. During the day, the temperature rises to 122°F (50°C) but it drops as soon as the sun sets.

DUST STORMS

A shamal *is a great dust storm that blows from the northwest across the Red Sea to the coastal areas of Yemen. It takes extremely high winds to create a dust storm. When the wind passes over areas of sparse vegetation, it picks up loose particles that can be as big as pieces of clay or as tiny as silt and fine sand. The particles are swept to heights of many feet, and the smaller ones can stay in the air for days. Some particles have even been found floating in the atmosphere above Alaska. Heavier grains of sand bounce along just a few inches above the ground.*

Sandstorms can be a real hazard. The sand particles carried by the wind act like sandpaper: They scrape away rock surfaces and remove paint from trucks. Dust storms can also erode valuable soil and destroy young crops.

During a shamal, *the wind can become so full of sand that it blocks out the sun, making visibility impossible. Each year airports have to close for a few days during July and August because the* shamal *clogs airplane engines. Similar dust storms occur in Sudan and in Egypt.*

FLORA

Yemen's plants are fascinating and often exceptionally beautiful. In the Western Highlands, there are flowering bushes of tamarisk, ficus, and acacia. The tiny yellow and white flowers of the acacia are often used for dyes. Fruit-bearing trees such as mango and papaya, as well as Yemen's famous coffee shrubs, also grow well here.

The Central Highlands region has almond, peach, and apricot trees and a variety of grapevines that grow along its terraced slopes.

Farther east, parts of the desert have no flora. Among the plants that have adapted to this arid region is the useful aloe; the dried juice of its leaves relieves sunburn.

In Yemen there grows the chewing gum tree. When the milky sap from the bark is left to dry in the sun, it develops a gumlike texture. Passersby peel it off and chew it.

Geography **13**

FRUIT OF THE DESERT

Throughout history, the date palm has played a vital role in the Middle East. It grows in areas where there is little water because it has long roots that can tap water sources far below the surface. In Yemen it flourishes around oases and in the Wadi Hadramawt. These trees can grow as tall as 92 feet (28 m). They start to bear fruit after four or five years and have been known to remain productive for up to 150 years. Each tree produces more than 1,000 dates in a single bunch. Yemen's date harvest is for both domestic consumption and export.

Dates are tasty and nourishing. They are rich in iron and other minerals, protein, fat, and vitamins. In addition to being a source of food, the date palm has many other uses: The trunks provide timber, the leaf ribs are used to make crates and furniture, and the smaller leaves are woven into beautiful baskets.

FAUNA

As recently as a century ago, Yemen had animals such as leopards, giraffes, pumas, oryx (large antelopes), and ibex (mountain goats). Sadly, the variety of wildlife has diminished because of hunting and population growth, which has resulted in the clearing of many natural habitats to make way for buildings. As of 2001, five mammal species and 13 bird species were listed as threatened.

Among the surviving animals are striped hyenas, caracals, hares, and foxes. One of the largest wild mammals still to be found in Yemen is the hamadryas baboon. Also called desert baboons, they travel together in groups. Found in the mountains, they are occasionally kept as pets and taken to the local markets for shows.

An Egyptian vulture perches on a boulder in Socotra's Haggier Mountains.

Despite a general lack of animal wildlife, Yemen has plenty of birds: 13 species are native to the country, and more than 400 species of migratory birds stop in Yemen on their way to Europe and Central Asia. In the highlands, there are ravens and vultures. Farther east, weaverbirds build their nests on telephone poles.

Yemen also has a fair share of insects, spiders, and reptiles. Desert locusts live in areas where rainfall is erratic, but they travel en masse in search of food. Each year swarms of desert locusts descend on farms and, within minutes, devour vital crops. Scorpions in the deserts and in some rocky parts of the highlands dart around grabbing small prey such as lizards. Desert reptiles, such as the desert viper, like to bask in the torrid heat, maintaining their body temperature by absorbing the heat of their surroundings.

CITIES

Yemen has thousands of small villages, and only about 26 percent of the population is urban based. As the economy grows and new industries develop, job opportunities attract rural migrants to the city centers. The main cities of Yemen are Sana'a, Aden, Ta'izz, and Hodeida.

Socotra has many indigenous birds. The sunbird, the grass-warbler, the mountain bunting, the sparrow, and the chestnut-winged starling are just a few of the island's birds.

Sana'a, the capital of Yemen, is believed to have been founded by Shem, one of Noah's sons, and is referred to in the Bible as Azal.

SANA'A

As the political capital of the Republic of Yemen, Sana'a is the largest and most important, as well as the oldest, city in Yemen. The name *Sana'a* means "Fortified Place." At one time, the Sabeans, who ruled over one of Yemen's ancient kingdoms, used it as a highland fortress.

Sana'a is famous for its exquisite architecture and for its medina, the old walled center of the city. Many of the buildings in the medina are more than 800 years old. But Sana'a is also a contemporary metropolis; it is this blend of ancient and modern that makes the capital so fascinating.

Since 1960 its population has increased rapidly. Its population stands at approximately 1,748,000 but is growing yearly. Christians and Jews used to live in Sana'a, but today its residents are almost exclusively Muslims.

ADEN

Aden (population: 800,000), built in the crater of an extinct volcano, is surrounded by huge lava mountains that shield the port from the elements, making it the best natural port in the Arabian Peninsula. Throughout history, Aden has been crucial to trade and transportation between the East and the West.

In 1839 Aden became a dependency of the British East India Company. As a result of the useful position of its port, which lies equidistant from the important ports of Zanzibar, Bombay (now Mumbai), and the Suez Canal, Aden served as a coaling station for the British. Aden remained under British rule until 1967.

After Yemen's unification in 1990, Aden was made the commercial capital and declared a free-trade zone.

An aerial view of Ta'izz in Yemen.

TA'IZZ Ta'izz (population: 460,000), Yemen's third-largest city, lies at the foot of Jabal Saber and sprawls over hills and lush green plains. The city is a thriving commercial center. Its markets are well known for their female merchants, who are admired for their fierce bargaining skills.

Compared with Sana'a and Aden, Ta'izz is a young city. It has a modern appearance, since most of its concrete buildings were built after 1962, the year the Yemen Arab Republic (YAR) was established. Despite its new look, some old quarters in the city and many lovely mosques remain.

HODEIDA In 1961 a disastrous fire destroyed much of the city of Hodeida. As Hodeida had been the site of a Soviet naval base in the 1970s and 1980s, the Soviets helped to rebuild and modernize the city, particularly its port, so that Soviet ships could make use of its facilities. Since then the city, which has a population of approximately 400,000, has continued to evolve, with concrete buildings and asphalt roads replacing the reed huts of local fishermen. The old Turkish quarter of the city remains intact, with handsome houses four stories high. The beautifully decorated doors of these houses were carved by Indian craftsmen who once accompanied traders to various ports.

HISTORY

Dar al-Hajar, a rock palace located in the Central Highlands, was built in the 1930s by Imam Yahya as a summer residence. The government now owns this remarkable place.

CHAPTER 2

T IS BELIEVED THAT AROUND 2000 B.C. descendants of Shem, a son of Noah, made inroads into what is now northwestern Yemen. They brought with them farming and building skills. About 1,000 years later, a great trading route developed. Caravans of camels laden with ivory, spices, incense, and textiles traveled through Yemen to the major markets of the ancient world.

The emergence of Islam in the seventh century was one of the most significant events in Yemen's history. Another historical turning point came much later, in 1990, when the northern and southern parts of the country merged to form the Republic of Yemen. Some of the period in between was marked by fighting between tribes and religious leaders, and against foreign invaders, including the British and the Ottoman Turks.

The ruins of the Ma'rib Dam are Yemen's most valuable archaeological site. Built by the Sabeans around 500 B.C., this dam irrigated the land and fed the people of early Yemen.

PRE-ISLAMIC CIVILIZATION

A caravan of pilgrims arrives at a fortress. Land routes were favored in historical times because the wind and currents of the Red Sea were too treacherous to navigate.

The earliest known civilization in southern Arabia began about 1000 B.C., when kingdoms based on five city-states flourished on the fringes of the eastern desert: Saba (also called Sheba), Qataban, Hadramawt, Awsan, and Ma'in. Each of these kingdoms appears to have enjoyed periods of prosperity, and they often coexisted. They also shared a similar faith based on polytheism, or the worship of many gods. The legendary kingdom of Saba, which lasted for at least 14 centuries, was probably the most powerful.

The kingdoms depended on agriculture and trade. Renowned for their brilliant building skills, the southern Arabians constructed ingenious dams and irrigation systems, enabling them to farm areas with little or no water.

The kingdoms became tremendously wealthy by trading with markets all over the ancient world. Southern Arabia was the source of two precious resins: frankincense and myrrh. Frankincense was burned as an incense offering to the ancient gods, and myrrh was an ingredient in cosmetics, perfumes, and curative treatments. These aromatics were highly valued by the ancient Greeks, Romans, and Egyptians. Besides trading their own goods, Yemeni merchants sold ivory from Africa, spices and textiles from India, and fine silk from China.

Goods were shipped from India and China across the Indian Ocean to the port of Aden. From there, camel caravans transported them along the Incense Road to the markets of Egypt, the Mediterranean countries, and Mesopotamia. So many riches poured out of southern Arabia at that time that the Greeks and Romans called it *Arabia Felix*, which is Latin for "Happy Arabia."

The kingdom of Saba, or Sheba, is best known for its legendary queen. The story of the queen of Sheba's visit to King Solomon appears in both the Old Testament and the Koran. In the story, a beautiful bird called a hoopoe brought news to King Solomon of the thriving kingdom of Saba and its queen. As queen of what may have been the most powerful kingdom in southern Arabia, she had great influence over the southern part of the Incense Road, while King Solomon controlled the northern end. Therefore it was vital to cement friendly relations.

In order to do so, the queen and her entourage traveled by camel all the way to the court of King Solomon in ancient Palestine. On arrival, she presented the king with an abundance of gifts, including spices, gold, and precious stones. Her mission was so successful and the king so charmed that she became known as Queen of the Arabs. This story has fascinated people of the East and the West ever since.

DECLINE OF THE KINGDOMS

In the first century A.D., when a Mediterranean seaman named Hippalus discovered a direct sea route between India and Egypt, the center of trade shifted westward to the coast of the Red Sea, where the kingdom of Himyar flourished. The caravan trails fell into disuse, and this loss of trade to India precipitated the decline of Saba. The whole of southern Arabia, including Yemen, became part of the Himyarite kingdom.

During the fourth and fifth centuries A.D., missionaries began converting the southern Arabian tribes to their own monotheistic faiths, and the old Sabean gods were forgotten. Several historians have suggested that these missionaries were mainly Christian immigrants or traders from Persia, who were escaping persecution in their homeland. Around the same time,

Christian and Jewish influences entered southern Arabia on the trade routes and across the Red Sea from the ancient kingdom of Ethiopia. Christianity was Ethiopia's official religion.

This tomb honors the memory of Queen Arwa in a mosque in the town of Jibla. After her husband died in 1067, Queen Arwa ruled the Sulayhid dynasty. She traveled widely in her state to encourage her people to abandon tribal quarrels and devote themselves to agriculture and development.

Christianity became the official religion of the Roman Empire. Demand for frankincense and myrrh plummeted as the church associated their use with pagan rituals, and the kingdoms of southern Arabia lost much of their wealth.

In A.D. 525 the king of Ethiopia seized Yemen. Forty-five years later, he attacked the kingdoms of Arabia but failed to conquer the region. He died soon after. After his death, the Himyarites enlisted the Persians' help to chase out the Ethiopians. When the Ethiopians were defeated in A.D. 575, the Himyarite kingdoms came under Persian rule.

THE SPREAD OF ISLAM

By the early seventh century A.D., a religion called Islam was introduced to the Arabian Peninsula by an Arab prophet born in A.D. 570 named Muhammad. The teachings of the prophet Muhammad spread rapidly, and the number of Islamic communities began to grow. By A.D. 628, the Persian governor of Yemen had converted to Islam. Everyone else in Yemen also converted.

After Muhammad died in A.D. 632, centuries of conflict followed, and a number of dynasties came and went. Among these were the Sulayhids, whose rulers included the exceptional Queen Arwa, and the Rasulids, who excelled in the arts and sciences.

The Zaidi Islamic sect established a state in northern Yemen in 897 when a descendant of the Prophet was invited to mediate a war between the Hashid and the Bakil tribes. Imam Yahya bin Husayn bin Qasim al-Rassi became the first political and religious ruler of the Zaidi dynasty. His teachings advocated an active political role for the imam, or religious leader. These principles laid the foundations of the Zaidi imamate that held power in Yemen for more than 1,000 years.

THE EUROPEANS AND THE FIRST OTTOMAN OCCUPATION

In the early 1500s the emerging powers of Europe became more interested in the lucrative trade between the Far East and the Mediterranean. Their attention became focused on controlling the Red Sea and Arabian coastal ports, which were vital arteries of the east—west trade. The Portuguese were the first to arrive. They annexed the island of Socotra in 1507, and in 1513 Afonso de Albuquerque, who had conquered Goa in India, tried unsuccessfully to take the port of Aden. Spurred on by the Portuguese attempt, the Mameluke rulers of Egypt subsequently mounted an attack on Aden but failed as well.

By 1517 the Ottoman Empire, centered in Turkey, had become the greatest military and naval power in the eastern Mediterranean and the Red Sea. To check Portuguese supremacy in the Indian Ocean, the Ottoman Turks arrived in Yemen. They conquered Ta'izz, Aden, and finally Sana'a in 1548.

During the Ottoman occupation, trade with Europe grew, and a great interest developed in the precious coffee beans grown in Yemen's highlands. The port of Mocha on the Red Sea became a pivotal point in the world coffee trade, attracting the English and the Dutch, who set up factories there.

The local population resented the occupation, and as early as 1590, one of the Zaidi imams, Qasim the Great, challenged the Turks. The armies that finally expelled the Turks in 1636 were drawn from northern tribesmen and led by Qasim's son, Muayyad Mohammed.

For more than 200 years, the Zaidi state extended its realm—east to the Wadi Hadramawt and as far north as the coastal region of Asir in what is now Saudi Arabia. Centralized control fell apart when some groups began to

Shaharah, a mountain town accessible only on foot, was the ideal headquarters for the Zaidi imams during the foreign occupation. This narrow bridge over a chasm separates it from the next town.

The watchtower in the old town of Ibb is part of the legacy of Yemen's colonial past.

claim independence. A turning point came when the sultan of Lahij, in the south, blocked Zaidi access to the port of Aden in 1728. The British had been scouring the coastline for a coaling station en route to India, and this proved to be a golden opportunity for them to increase their influence in the area.

THE BRITISH IN SOUTH YEMEN

In the 19th century a number of developments enabled Great Britain to expand its global realm. The development of the steam engine and railroads in the 1830s made transportation more efficient, and the ports of the Mediterranean and the Red Sea became connected to the ports of London and Liverpool in England. With the increasing activities of the British East India Company, Aden became an even more important port of call for ships and steamships on the route between Europe and India.

In 1839 the British took over Aden. It was ruled by the British East India Company until 1937, when it became a British crown colony. To protect Aden from a Turkish takeover, the British drew up a number of protection treaties with the local sheikhs, or tribal leaders. In return for British military protection, the sheikhs promised not to transfer their territory without British consent. In this way, Great Britain's Protectorate of South Arabia was formed.

Under British rule, the port of Aden gained in size and importance. It benefited from political stability, improved commercial policies, and updated harbor facilities. Aden became a center for the transshipment of goods and a hub of trading activity, surpassing the traditional ports of the Arabian and Red Sea coasts.

THE SECOND OTTOMAN OCCUPATION

In the mid-19th century the Ottoman Turks reappeared as a major influence in the Red Sea region. This event led to a Turkish takeover of northern Yemen. The Ottomans began by reestablishing their authority in the Tihama in 1849, to forestall British control of the entire Red Sea. The opening of the Suez Canal in 1869 prompted the Turks to expand into the highlands. They began occupying the major cities, finally capturing the Zaidi capital of Sa'da in 1882.

This magnificent Turkish mausoleum in Ta'izz was built during the Ottoman Empire.

Ottoman and British interests clashed. Both powers agreed to demarcate boundaries between them and drew a border between north and south in 1905. This sealed the division between North Yemen and South Yemen, a division that lasted until unification in 1990.

The local population opposed the Turkish occupation, and there were a number of uprisings by the Zaidis as well as by the northern Tihama tribes under the leadership of Sayyid Mohammed al-Idrisi. In 1904 Imam Yahya ibn Mohammed organized a resistance movement among the highland Yemenis. Under the 1911 Treaty of Da'an, he finally forced the Turks to accept a division of power granting him autonomy in the highlands.

After the Ottoman Empire's defeat in World War I in 1918, the Turks withdrew from North Yemen. The Treaty of Lausanne officially ended Turkish rule, and North Yemen obtained international recognition as an independent state ruled by the powerful Imam Yahya. South Yemen remained in the hands of the British.

CONSOLIDATION OF THE ZAIDI IMAMATE

After gaining independence, Imam Yahya set about consolidating central authority and securing the borders. In the Tihama in 1925, he conquered the Idrisi forces, who then allied themselves with Saudi Arabia. Yahya's northern advances alarmed the Saudis, culminating in the Saudi-Yemeni War of 1934. This ended with the Taif Treaty, leaving Asir and Najran temporarily under Saudi rule. These territories are still in dispute today.

Fearing that outside contact might result in challenges to his authority, Imam Yahya decided on a policy of isolation. His efforts were aided by North Yemen's agriculturally self-sufficient economy. At a time when the rest of the Arab world was modernizing, Yemen turned inward.

Nevertheless Imam Yahya realized that to be secure, he needed foreign technology, particularly military, and this required education and training. In the 1930s the first Yemenis went abroad to be educated. Once exposed to foreign ideas, however, they began to question Imam Yahya's leadership. In 1948 a group of liberal reformers, led by Abdullah al-Wazzir, assassinated Imam Yahya, but Yahya's son, Imam Ahmad, drove them out. Later, Imam Ahmad established his own government, which closely resembled that of his father.

Imam Ahmad ruled Yemen after the assassination of his father, Imam Yahya.

FORMATION OF THE YEMEN ARAB REPUBLIC

Following Imam Ahmad's death in 1962, his son Muhammad al-Badr came to power. Within a week, a group of army officers staged a coup, deposed him, and proclaimed North Yemen to be the Yemen Arab Republic (YAR), with Colonel Abdullah Sallal as the president. Imam al-Badr fled to the northern mountains and organized forces to help him restore his regime. The country plunged into civil war. Egypt and the Soviet Union supported the republicans, while Saudi Arabia and Britain backed the imam's royalists.

Imam Ahmad had tremendous personality—he was shrewd, well educated, amusing, suspicious, and often terrifying. He dealt severely with dissidents and was feared by his subjects, who believed that he possessed supernatural powers. The imam played upon the public fear of his alleged psychic powers by making it known that he communicated with the spirit world. His servants claimed that they could hear him talking to the jinn, or spirits, when he was alone in his room. His subjects also believed he possessed power over poisonous snakes that warned him of plots threatening his life. Imam Ahmad's efforts to cultivate a fear of his power did not deter the hostile forces against him, which included some tribal chiefs and members of the intelligentsia.

By 1967 the fighting had reached an impasse. The royalists faced defeat, and internal conflict troubled the republican ranks. As a result, the Egyptians withdrew their troops, and Abdul Rahman al-Iryani replaced Sallal as president. The civil war finally ended in 1970 when Imam al-Badr was exiled to Britain. The republicans established a government that lasted until 1974, when a group of army leaders took control and steered the country in a conservative direction.

THE PEOPLE'S DEMOCRATIC REPUBLIC OF YEMEN

The 1960s were turbulent times for South Yemen as well. Around the same time that Imam al-Badr was being overthrown, South Yemen was undergoing a socialist revolution.

Despite opposition in 1963 the British made Aden a crown colony to be included in its protectorate the Federation of South Arabia. Although Britain promised to grant independence to the federation at a later date, nationalism had already swept through the south. Among the nationalist groups a left-wing rebel movement known as the National Liberation Front (NLF) was organized and began a campaign of terror.

The Federation of South Arabia finally collapsed in 1967, forcing the British to withdraw. The NLF declared South Yemen independent. In 1970 it

British air forces in Yemen during the war of independence.

became the People's Democratic Republic of Yemen (PDRY) under the leadership of President Qahtan al-Shabi. Eventually the NLF developed into the Yemeni Socialist Party (YSP).

The economy of the new republic was in shambles. In the late 1960s the country suffered from a long drought. What's more, the closure of the Suez Canal in 1967 aggravated the effects of the loss of British trade and investment and further reduced Aden's economic role in the world. These factors led to widespread hunger, economic hardship, social problems, and even deaths in many parts of the country. The PDRY managed to stay afloat only with financial aid from the Soviet Union and other communist countries of Eastern Europe.

To make matters worse, an internal ideological power struggle threatened the country's political stability. Political sentiment became more left-wing and even more closely allied with the communist bloc. In 1969 President al-Shabi was ousted in favor of President Salim Rubayi Ali, who brought most of the economy under government control.

UNIFICATION OF THE TWO YEMENS

At the beginning of the 1970s both the YAR and the PDRY relied on foreign aid to revive their war-damaged economies. Saudi Arabia and Western Europe supported the YAR, while the PDRY was aided by the Soviet Union. Strained relations resulted in a series of wars along their border.

In 1978, after a succession of leaders, Colonel Ali Abdullah Saleh became president of the YAR. He embraced a Western-style market economy. During the 1980s the economy grew stronger under his rule.

Meanwhile in the PDRY, a civil war broke out in 1986 when the views of extreme Marxists clashed with those of the government. Around the same time financial aid dried up with the collapse of the Soviet Union. Bankrupt, the PDRY turned to its northern neighbor for help.

This monument marks the unification of North and South Yemen as the Republic of Yemen.

Previously there had been unification talks between the two Yemens, but the discovery of oil in the desert bordering both countries sped up the process. They finally merged in May 22, 1990. Saleh became president, and a southerner, Ali Salim al-Baydh, became vice president.

The first few years for the new nation were filled with trouble. A disagreement between supporters of the president and those of the vice president resulted in a civil war in 1994. But within a few months, troops supporting the president won the war, and the country remained united. Although Yemen remains a unified country, some cultural differences between regional groups in the north and the south continue to exist.

YEMEN AFTER UNIFICATION

Today Yemen enjoys a degree of relative peace and stability, although there are incidents of tourist kidnappings and other acts of terrorism. It has managed to establish a democratic system. Although the discovery of oil and the increase in oil prices in 2000 boosted the government's revenues, Yemen still remains one of the poorest countries in the Middle East.

GOVERNMENT

The Sultan's Palace in Wadi Hadramawt.

CHAPTER 3

THE FORMATION OF THE REPUBLIC of Yemen on May 22, 1990, was one of the most momentous occasions in the history of Yemen. At last, the people of both Yemens had become a part of one state.

Yemen's political system is unique in the Arabian Peninsula. The people wanted a democratic system of government based on direct popular elections, freedom of speech, and an independent judiciary. The struggle for democracy came from the people's desire to end absolute rule.

THE CONSTITUTION

Before unification, the two Yemens had different political systems. The YAR was a republic, ruled under a provisional constitution dating back to the 1970s, although successive governing bodies exercised little real power until the 1980s. In contrast, the PDRY favored Marxist principles; government policy was determined by the Yemeni Socialist Party.

Once both Yemens had agreed to unite, the legislatures of both the YAR and also the PDRY then approved a draft constitution for the new nation. This constitution was a major deviation from the previous two. Despite the opposition from certain factions,

Crowds of armed antigovernment protesters hold up flags of the former South Yemen during a protest in the southern Yemeni city of Yafaa.

Yemeni president Ali Abdullah Saleh (*center*) poses for a group picture with members of the new cabinet at the presidential palace in Sana'a.

the majority of the population supported the constitution in a popular referendum in mid-May 1991. Yemen was governed by this constitution until October 1, 1994, when some amendments were made.

The revised constitution defines the Republic of Yemen as "an independent and sovereign Arab and Islamic country." It states that the republic "is an indivisible whole, and it is impermissible to concede any part of it. The Yemeni people are part of the Arab and Islamic nation." The revised constitution stipulates that sharia, which is the Islamic law, is the source of all law. Sharia is an interpretation of the reading of the Koran, as well as an interpretation of the sayings and actions of the prophet Muhammad.

A further amendment abolished the five-member presidential council, which included the president and the vice president. The president's position is now stronger because the people elect him directly.

THE INSTITUTIONS OF GOVERNMENT

The constitution set out a parliamentary system of government based on direct popular elections. Anyone who is over 18 years of age can vote. The Assembly of Representatives is the legislative branch of the state. Yemen has a two-part, or mixed, legislature: a lower house called the House of

Not everybody embraced the original constitution wholeheartedly. Among those who opposed it were religious groups in the north, including the Muslim Brotherhood. They objected strongly to the proposed constitution and urged the rest of the population to boycott it because it was not based exclusively on Islamic law.

The Muslim Brotherhood was founded in Egypt in 1928, and it has grown to be one of the largest and most influential Islamist groups in the world today. It preaches social justice and the eradication of poverty and corruption. The Muslim Brotherhood opposes the use of violence and is particularly against colonialism by the Western countries.

In the south, there were demonstrations by women. Afraid that their freedom might be jeopardized if Islamic sentiments became too extreme, they demanded that their rights be guaranteed in the new constitution.

All objections were thwarted when the leaders of both Yemens proclaimed unification on May 22, 1990, six months ahead of schedule. The Republic of Yemen was born with Sana'a as its political capital and Aden as the economic center. President Ali Abdullah Saleh was selected to lead the people into a new era.

Representatives and an upper house called the Shura Council. *Shura* is Arabic for "consultative." The president created the Shura Council in May 1997.

The lower house consists of 301 elected members who serve for six-year terms. The upper house is made up of 111 members who are appointed by the president. This two-part legislature in Yemen means that power is shared between the two houses, and a concurrent majority must be achieved in order to pass any legislation. The Assembly of Representatives is responsible for enacting laws, approving policies and development plans, supervising public spending, and ratifying international treaties. The president cannot dissolve it, except in an emergency.

The president and a cabinet of ministers make up the executive branch. The president is elected for a seven-year term by popular vote. He is empowered to appoint the vice president, the prime minister, and other ministers on the advice of the prime minister.

Members of Yemen's parliament during a meeting in Sana'a.

The issue of local government is still under discussion, but Yemen is currently divided into 19 administrative units known as governorates, sometimes called provinces. Headed by governors, these governorates are divided into smaller units known as districts and local councils. The local government administers various aspects of community life, such as health, education, and tax collection.

THE LEGAL SYSTEM

The principles of Islam concern all aspects of life, and Islam provides its followers with a means of ordering their daily lives according to the will of Allah (God). Muslims believe that God's words were revealed through the prophet Muhammad and later became the Koran, the holy book of Islam. These sacred writings were supplemented by a collection of Muhammad's sayings known as the Hadith. Together they form the basis of sharia ("God's way"), which is an interpretation of the law of Islam. Sharia includes a range of rules governing behavior. These include religious rituals such as prayer, family matters such as marriage, and how a Muslim should behave in society. In addition to sharia, the tribes have their own unwritten customary laws relating to standards of good behavior and social conduct. Sunni Muslims have their own interpretations of the Koran and their own set of rules governing behavior.

The state and the judiciary are separate within Yemen's legal system. This means that judges can carry out their duties independently, and the courts have the power to decide all disputes and crimes. The law is the only authority that governs their work.

The structure of the courts is consistent with the administrative divisions of the country. Every district has a court of first instance, which tries civil, criminal, matrimonial, and commercial cases. Every governorate has a court of appeal that looks into appeals against the decisions of the district courts. The Supreme Court, located in the capital city of Sana'a, is the highest court of appeal in the land. Headed by a chief justice with a bench of seven judges under him, the Supreme Court looks into appeals against decisions of the courts of appeal.

Yemeni soldiers march during a military parade. Apart from an army, navy, and air force, there is also a paramilitary force in Yemen.

POLITICAL PARTIES AND CIVIL WAR

This monument was built to honor the people who lost their lives during the civil war.

Following unification, more than 40 new parties vied for popular support. The first election, held in April 27, 1993, drew enthusiastic voters. The result was a three-party coalition: the General People's Congress (GPC), formerly dominant in the north; the Yemeni Socialist Party (YSP), formerly dominant in the south; and the Yemeni Congregation for Reform, also known as the Islah Party, which represented tribal and Islamic interests. Yemen became the first multiparty state in the Arabian Peninsula.

Soon after the election, clouds began to gather. A disagreement over the sharing of power between the GPC, led by President Ali Abdullah Saleh, and the YSP, led by Ali Salim al-Baydh, pushed the country to the brink of disaster in 1993. A full-blown civil war broke out on May 4, 1994.

Shortly after the war began, al-Baydh proclaimed the independent Democratic Republic of Yemen, hoping to win the support of those countries on the Arabian Peninsula that did not support Saleh. However, Saleh's troops surrounded Aden, and the secessionists, including al-Baydh, fled to other parts of the Arab world.

After the YSP's defeat, President Saleh affirmed his commitment to democracy. To prevent future uprisings, he declared that party membership would no longer be allowed within the armed forces. To foster reconciliation, most secessionists who put down their weapons were granted amnesty. Despite its brevity, the civil war was a blow to the fragile economy and tipped the political balance of power. The YSP lost influence, and a coalition between the GPC and the Islah Party ruled until April 1997, when the GPC won a majority. Since then the government has assumed more influence over the opposition and the media.

PRESIDENT SALEH

President Ali Abdullah Saleh was born in 1942 in the village of Bait al-Ahmar in the Sana'a governorate, where he attended a Koranic school for his elementary education. In 1958 he joined the armed forces and, to continue his studies, enrolled in the noncommissioned officers' school in 1960.

President Saleh had a long and successful military career in which he was promoted through the ranks. He attended various service schools, assumed a number of posts, and in 1983 attained the rank of colonel. The former president of North Yemen, he assumed office as president of the Republic of Yemen after unification in 1990. As president, he is commander-in-chief of the armed forces.

President Saleh won the 1999 election by an overwhelming majority, although there were angry opposition boycotts, claims of vote rigging, and violence at polling booths that left many Yemenis injured or dead.

In February 2009 the Assembly of Representatives approved a two-year postponement of its legislative elections. This was an attempt to calm heightening tensions between the governing party and the opposition over the fairness of elections. The elections were scheduled for April 2009 but will now take place in April 2011.

Today Yemen is a dominant-party state, with the General People's Congress in power. Opposition parties exist but are widely considered to have little chance of gaining real power. Besides the governing GPC, the other main parties are the Islah Party, the Yemen Socialist Party, the Nasserite Unionist People's Organization, and the Arab Socialist Rebirth Party.

The Islah Party, which was formed in 1990, has two branches: tribal and religious. Islah's political focus is on the relationship between Islam and the state and the issues of religious education.

There is quite a female force behind Islah, Yemen's largest Islamic party. Islah in Arabic means "reform" or "repair." Although the Islah Party does not have any female candidates, women work behind the scenes. They come from varied backgrounds, but quite a few are university graduates. Most of them are in their late teens or early twenties and do not have children yet. The majority of them are religious and consider the work they do for the party as part of their religious duty.

Islahi women are involved in a number of social activities that bring them into daily contact with other women in society. There are religious study groups, women's committees, women's centers, charities, and various other women's organizations. Many of these activities are just part of the Yemeni way of life, but they provide Islahi women with an opportunity to educate other women about the Islah Party in order to gain their support. In the course of their daily contact with other women, Islahi women have contributed to the success of the Islah Party.

POLITICAL OUTLOOK

In recent years President Saleh has remained steadfast in his efforts to improve economic conditions and foreign relations. The international community supported his government's implementation of an economic reform program and rewarded it with aid. Nevertheless the austere economic policies have resulted in domestic protests. In particular, the removal of energy subsidies, which increased the price of fuel, resulted in a confrontation between the army and farmers.

In 1992 tensions between Yemen and Saudi Arabia increased because of a dispute over an oil field near the Saudi-Yemeni border. Both countries agreed to negotiations in mid-1992. Relations have since become more amicable, and Yemen and Saudi Arabia have expressed their commitment to improving economic, commercial, and cultural cooperation. In June 1995 President Saleh made a successful visit to Saudi Arabia. Finally, following the Treaty of Jiddah in 2000, a border agreement with Saudi Arabia was signed in 2006 , bringing long-standing disputes between the two countries to an end. Today Yemen has no outstanding disputes with any of its neighbors.

CONTEMPORARY POLITICAL CRITICISM

The people of Yemen, particularly the younger and more educated generation, are finding new ways, such as blogging, to voice their political views and to obtain information and news that is banned from being published or broadcast in Yemen's state-owned media. Although it is hard to determine the precise number, there are thousands of Yemeni bloggers, most of whom use the popular Arabic blogger platform of Maktoobblog.com. In 2008 the Ministry of Foreign Affairs blocked several popular blogging platforms and even arrested some political bloggers who criticized the government. As a result, the Yemeni government has faced some international criticism.

Since unification, various political parties have emerged in Yemen. One of the newest political parties, which established itself in 2009, is the Liberation Party—Yemen Rule. The party's ideology calls on the country to adopt a caliphate system that complies with shariah. The party preaches an Islamic lifestyle and the spread of Islam to the world.

Yemen is a member of the United Nations, the Arab League, and the Organization of Islamic Conference.

Yemeni women dressed in traditional attire wait outside a polling station to cast their ballots during an election.

ECONOMY

A farmer stands amid his crops in Yemen.

CHAPTER 4

THROUGHOUT HISTORY, most Yemenis have been farmers. In modern times, Yemen's economy has been largely dependent on foreign aid and the wages sent home by Yemenis who work in other Arab countries.

Since the discovery of oil in the 1980s, earnings from oil production and the Aden refinery have significantly contributed to Yemen's income. Even with its oil resources, however, Yemen remains one of the poorest countries of the Arabian Peninsula.

In 2008 the slowdown in the world economy and the decrease in the price of oil adversely affected Yemen's economy growth. With oil resources slowly diminishing, Yemen has some serious challenges to overcome in order to revive its economy. To reduce its reliance on oil exports and international aid, Yemen has begun a program of reform and diversification. For example, a facility to liquefy natural gas was being built to open in 2009. Apart from diversification, it is looking to strengthen both its physical and its political infrastructure and combat widespread corruption.

A Yemeni man works with iron in Sana'a.

THE CHALLENGE OF DEVELOPMENT

With unification, Yemen inherited two opposing economic systems. The former YAR operated a Western-style economy with very little government interference. The PDRY was centrally planned; its government decided how and what to produce and who would receive the goods. Both were economically similar, however, in that they were inward-looking and reliant on foreign aid and remittances from Yemeni workers abroad. After unification, the YAR system was adopted.

AGRICULTURE

Agriculture contributes around 9 percent of Yemen's gross domestic product (GDP). Much of its agricultural activities depend on rain, but the rains are temperamental, challenging farmers to construct ingenious irrigation systems to catch the water. The highlands are covered with exquisite terraces that prevent fertile soil from being washed away. Some farmers now use

A young shepherdess tends to her goats in the village of al-Mashad.

Much of Yemen's landscape is paved with terraced farmlands.

diesel pumps to run water to their fields, so whenever fuel prices are raised, there is a public outcry. The Yemen authorities have invested in building dams and modern irrigation systems to increase the availability of water for agricultural use.

Although the society is becoming less agrarian, agriculture is still the primary occupation of more than three-quarters of the population. Households farm small plots of land that produce very little. Each year fewer people farm and less food is produced.

Once self-sufficient in food, Yemen now depends on imports. One reason is that working for wages abroad or in the cities has become an attractive alternative to working in the fields. This reduces the labor force available for farming and therefore leads to less produce. On the other hand, the resulting income has helped to diversify the economy. When the men return to their villages, some of them have saved enough money to open shops. Others invest in a truck and shuttle villagers back and forth for a fee.

Another reason food imports are needed is that more khat, a shrub whose leaves are chewed for their stimulating effect, is being grown as a cash crop at the expense of food crops. Because of the high local demand, a large number of farmers have converted their land to khat fields. The growing of khat is

MOCHA COFFEE

Two hundred years ago Yemen supplied all of Europe with coffee. It was shipped from the port of Mocha, hence the name mocha coffee. Even after competitors entered the market, coffee remained Yemen's primary source of foreign exchange. Since the 1970s, however, coffee production has been declining because more farmers are growing khat.

But coffee could make a comeback. In Western markets, mocha is associated with good coffee. It has a strong aroma and is perfect for blending with other beans. Coffee lovers are particularly fond of the delicious mocha-java combination. Attempts to boost coffee production began in the 1980s, with a Ministry of Agriculture development project designed to discover how to increase the yield per acre. Although African and Latin American plantations can produce cheaper coffee, Yemen has a competitive advantage when it comes to the taste.

In Yemen, as in many other countries around the world, drinking coffee provides a focus at social gatherings. As in other Arab countries, the making and serving of coffee in Yemen constitutes a significant part of showing hospitality to one's guests. There are rituals and skills associated with coffee making and preparation that include roasting the coffee beans and mixing the coffee with fragrant spices.

A popular drug with the locals, khat is grown and sold all over in Yemen.

controversial because Yemen is a poor country, yet half of its land is used to grow this cash crop. What's more, khat is addictive, and its use has been linked to long-term health issues such as heart problems and mental illness.

Although women chew khat, its use is more prevalent among the men. Many families spend a large portion of their income on khat and a fair amount of their time chewing it. This habit used to be confined to the rich elite, but it became affordable to the rest of society when incomes rose. It is claimed that up to 90 percent of the population are chewing this drug for up to five hours a day.

Nonetheless, Yemen's agricultural output is quite varied. It includes grains such as sorghum, corn, wheat, barley, and millet, and vegetables and legumes such as radishes, onions, beans, lentils, and leeks. Fruits include mangoes, bananas, apricots, and grapes from the Central Highlands, while dates for export are grown in the Wadi Hadramawt. Northern Yemen is renowned for its honey and mocha coffee. Nonfood crops, in addition to khat, include tobacco and cotton.

Most rural families breed livestock for milk and meat. Women herd cows, and children tend sheep and goats, which provide wool and hides. In recent years farmers have also been rearing chickens in commercial farms as the demand for eggs has grown.

Coffee is native to northern Yemen; Kenya, and Ethiopia. All three countries have similar flora and fauna because they were part of the same landmass until a rift created the Red Sea.

Besides working on their farms, most Yemeni women also take their home-grown produce to the markets to sell.

WOMEN IN AGRICULTURE When men left for better-paying jobs abroad or in the cities, some of them were able to send enough money home so that women could purchase appliances to lighten the housekeeping load. Still, many rural women carry an extra burden. Rural women from poorer economic backgrounds are often up at the crack of dawn, cooking for the family and feeding the animals. They might have to collect firewood or fetch water, a back-breaking task when it involves a climb into the mountains. Then they tackle the farmwork—sowing seeds, weeding fields, spraying pesticides, plowing, and harvesting. In some families, even old women perform light tasks. For those whose everyday chores are heavy, there is less free time available for them to do the things they enjoy.

A number of government projects are now in place to help these women produce more with less effort, so that they can have more free time even as they increase their income. The World Economic Forum's 2008 Gender Gap Report ranked Yemen as having the greatest inequality between women and men out of 130 countries.

NATURAL RESOURCES

The rich fishing waters around Yemen are the country's least developed natural resource. The Red and Arabian seas are full of mackerel, squid, shrimp, lobster, cuttlefish, and tuna. Most fishermen are small-scale entrepreneurs who lack the money to buy more efficient equipment. Even if more fish were caught, there would not be sufficient processing plants to turn the fish into a valuable export.

The discovery of oil reserves in the 1980s brightened Yemen's economic prospects. Commercial extraction began in 1986. Oil wells were opened, and pipelines were built to transport the oil from the fields to the coast. Recently, though, oil production has been gradually declining. Between 2001 and 2007, oil production decreased from 438,500 to 320,600 barrels per day (bpd). However, the Yemeni government made plans to increase production from 2009.

Yemen has a lot to offer the tourist: a good climate, stunning landscapes with untouched beaches, scuba-diving sites, a cultural heritage with fabulous architecture, and no shortage of historical sites to explore. Yemeni hospitality is unmatched, and the country's customs are fascinating. With sufficient funds and appropriate government guidance, tourist revenue could be a more significant source of income.

To encourage foreign and local investment, the government has modernized business and tourist facilities such as hotels, convention centers, and restaurants. Many, however, are still below international standards. Tourism is also hampered by weak infrastructure, unreliable transportation networks, and security concerns. In 2000 and 2002, the port at Aden was attacked by terrorists with bombs. Fifteen people were killed and 55 were injured in a bomb blast at the Bin Salman Mosque in May 2008. In September 2008 a car bomb exploded outside the U.S. embassy in Sana'a, and in November 2008 a bomb exploded aboard a minibus at the capital's al-Hasha station.

Another obstacle to the growth of tourism is kidnapping. Some foreigners who have strayed from the beaten track have been kidnapped by tribesmen, who use the hostages to increase their bargaining power with the central government. Some of these victims have been treated rather well, though, and plied with local drinks and delicacies.

An oil refinery in Aden.

Yemen mines substantial quantities of salt and marble. Because the country's unique architectural styles require cement, stone, alabaster, and marble, local demand for these commodities is very high.

INDUSTRY

The industrial sector in Yemen accounts for 47 percent of the national output. Oil refining is the most important industry, generating 40 percent of total revenue. The construction industry is growing, along with the manufacture of bricks, tiles, and other building materials. Other manufactured goods include consumer goods, food products such as flour and cooking oil, bottled soft drinks, aluminum houseware products, rubber and plastic products including water storage tanks, and doors and windows.

The service sector, mainly government and trade services, accounts for 40 percent of Yemen's national output. Public service, distribution, packing, shipping, insurance services, and tourism are expanding.

As in most other developing countries, several deficiencies are constraining industrial development in Yemen: Supplies of water and energy are unreliable, the local workforce lacks industrial expertise, and the transportation network is inefficient, with no guarantee that goods are delivered to factories and markets on time.

Like many other economically developing countries, Yemen has relied heavily on its human resources for economic wealth. Yemeni workers were the country's main export for much of the 20th century. These workers found employment primarily in Saudi Arabia and other Arab states. It is estimated that the remittances sent back to the country by hardworking Yemenis abroad amounted to $3 billion. Their families used this money to buy goods and services, thus helping to boost Yemen's economy. In 1990 Saudi Arabia withdrew the rights of Yemenis to work in the country and cut off its aid to Yemen, in protest against Yemen's ambiguous stand on Saddam Hussein's invasion of Kuwait, an action that caused the Gulf War. This forced 850,000 Yemenis to return home, which resulted in a massive loss of revenue, record unemployment levels, and economic chaos.

Yemen's economy is still suffering from the negative effects of Saudi Arabia's action, as well as from the 1994 civil war. Accustomed to relying on the hard work and hard currency earned by its army of workers abroad, the country has not completely succeeded in building a vibrant economy, even with the support of foreign aid.

ENERGY AND TRANSPORTATION

Businesses and households need electric power. Energy is needed to run industrial machinery and household appliances. In Yemen there is not enough energy to go around, so it is expensive, and supplies are unreliable. Locally produced petroleum meets some energy requirements, but the country is still reliant on imported fuel and energy. Until the 1960s Sana'a had no electricity, but now nearly everyone in Sana'a has it. Supplying electricity to some remote rural areas is costly, so these areas have to rely on local generators.

To develop the economy, expand its non-oil sectors, and improve the well-being of the people, Yemen needs foreign aid to improve health, education, roads, and water supplies and to develop agriculture. This money, in the form of loans or grants, comes from international donors such as the International Monetary Fund, the World Bank, the European Union, and the United Nations. Economic aid between 2003 and 2007 stood at $2.3 billion. Yemen also tries to encourage foreign investment by offering attractive incentives to potential investors.

ENVIRONMENT

Clouds swirl around the peaks of the
Haggier Mountains on Socotra Island.

A S WITH MANY OTHER COUNTRIES, economic growth in Yemen has been achieved at the expense of the environment. Land in Yemen has been intensively farmed and animals hunted to the extent that most of the natural flora and fauna have been destroyed.

When Yemeni laborers migrated elsewhere for work, they abandoned terraced fields, and it took only a few years to wash away fertile soil from the neglected land. As a result, Yemen now experiences severe problems with desertification.

On top of their other chores, these women also fetch clean water for their families.

A recent but pressing problem that has developed in Yemen is the dangerous shortage of water in rural as well as urban areas. As more pumps are being used for irrigation and household use, the level of groundwater is depleting at an alarming rate. In many parts of the country, access to fresh drinking water is limited, which makes daily life a challenge for the people of Yemen. The lack of water also causes diseases and problems with hygiene, jeopardizing the health of the population. Fortunately a water resource program has been developed with the help of international donors. Yemen also faces problems with water pollution due to contamination from oil production, untreated sewage, and salination.

Climate change has already caused major problems in Yemen and has contributed to a growing shortage of food in the country. In fact, if things do not improve soon, Yemen may face a very real food crisis.

Tourism also poses some environmental problems, but it is not a major issue as yet. There is a chance that proper planning can help prevent further environmental degradation.

The beautiful blue Indian Ocean off Socotra Island.

Lush greenery such as this is fast becoming a rare sight in Yemen.

At present, Yemen is a party to the International Biodiversity, Climate Change, Desertification, Endangered Species, Environmental Modification, Hazardous Wastes, Law of the Sea, Nuclear Test Ban, and Ozone Layer Protection agreements.

SOIL EROSION AND DESERTIFICATION

Although agriculture plays an important role in Yemen's economy, its natural environment does not always help support it. Yemen regularly experiences fierce sandstorms and dust storms that cause soil erosion and heavy damage to precious agricultural crops.

Yemen was once covered by lush forests and woodland, but its forested areas have gradually been depleted by overgrazing by goats and other animals. The brutal destruction of forests and trees for use as fuel and in the construction industry has also contributed to the problem. The implications of desertification directly affect agricultural workers and indirectly bring problems to the general Yemeni population. The most serious consequences

Desertification continues to be a major problem for Yemen.

of desertification include growing hunger among the population, poor health, and continued poverty. The problem is so serious that in 2004, Yemen established a national plan to fight against further desertification. This plan has received the support of the Yemeni government and its international partners, including the United Nations desertification program. Unfortunately, for various reasons, including lack of financial support, poor organization, and low rainfall over many years, not all the aims set out in the national plan to prevent desertification have been accomplished. The people of Yemen continue to struggle against the effects of desertification today. Yemeni farmers try to combat the problem of desertification by constructing hillside terraces, which can help to reduce soil erosion and conserve water.

THE WATER CRISIS

Yemen is a semiarid country with no permanent river systems, only seasonal ones. The country has a comparatively low rainfall of 20 to 31.5 inches (500 to 800 mm) a year. In ancient times, Yemen was the envy of the rest of the Arabian Peninsula for being a lush green land. Since the mid-1990s, however, Yemen's water resources have been slowly depleting. This has been caused mainly by overuse by the agricultural sector, climate change, and a population that is one of the fastest growing in the world. Today Yemen is suffering from a dangerous scarcity of water.

The National Water Resources Authority (NWRA) of Yemen estimates that the total renewable freshwater resources for the country are just 88,287 million cubic feet (2,500 million cubic m) a year. The current demand, however, is reported to be 113,007 million cubic feet (3,200 cubic m) a year, which indicates a deficit of 24,720 million cubic feet (700 million cubic m). As the population keeps growing, the deficit will continue to widen, making the situation even worse.

This Yemeni woman goes to the communal well for her daily water supply.

The capital city of Sana'a has experienced an astonishing population boom in recent times. In 1975 the city's population was 135,000. Today it stands at nearly 1.75 million and is predicted to continue to grow by as much as 8 percent a year. This explosion in the city's population has unsurprisingly put heavy demands on its resources and basic services, in particular water. In the Sana'a basin, water levels are dropping by 20 feet (6 m) a year. As the municipal services struggle to meet the city's demands for water, many city dwellers resort to buying their water from private sources, and many private residential estates have installed their own water supplies. In an attempt to provide more water to the city, the authorities have been forced to turn to the city's ancient aquifers. To reach the water found in them, workers had to dig deep wells in Sana'a. The average depth of wells in most countries is around 656 feet (200 m), but in Sana'a wells are as deep as 3,937 feet (1,200 m) to reach the aquifers. Even with such extreme measures being taken, it is estimated that the water in Sana'a will run out in 15 to 20 years.

Agricultural production is a significant contributor to Yemen's economy, accounting for almost 10 percent of national output. More important, the agricultural sector provides precious jobs for a large percentage of the country's population. The scarcity of water greatly hurts agricultural production. Due to the high demand and profitability associated with the growing of khat, an increasing number of agricultural workers are demanding the use of more and more water for irrigating their khat crops. This increase in demand puts pressure on an already diminished supply of water. As a result of the poor management of water resources, the water crisis continues in the agricultural sector.

Unfortunately the water shortages are experienced not just in the rural agricultural community. Due to a growing migration of people from rural to urban areas, the towns and cities in Yemen also face pressing water problems. Urban dwellers who need water for drinking and other domestic uses are competing with their rural neighbors for the precious supply. In Sana'a a mere 15 to 25 percent of residents are able to obtain drinking water from the city's official water system. The rest are forced to look elsewhere. The majority purchase their water from private vendors who can be found in the city's streets selling water that they have sourced from private wells as well as from the villages surrounding the city. There are plans to build a series of dams to solve the water shortage. Many fear, however, that this solution is not feasible, as building these dams is prohibitively expensive. The scarcity of water and the poor water quality will damage public health and more than likely make everyday living more difficult for the majority of Yemenis.

THE EFFECTS OF CLIMATE CHANGE

Like many other countries around the world, Yemen has been seriously affected by climate change, including changes in rainfall patterns and a longer period of low temperatures. In the past, the rainy season used to begin at the start of March. Now, however, it is common for Yemen not to receive rainfall until as late as the end of April. This lack of rainfall is a huge problem for Yemen, causing great hardships especially for its agricultural workers and industries where much water is needed.

A boy drinks from a freshwater source in Yemen.

With such rapid climate change, Yemen's gorgeous wadis, such as this one on Socotra island, could be under threat.

For example, its grain production has declined drastically. This is a significant problem as it not only reduces the availability of food to Yemen's growing population but also endangers the livelihood of a large portion of its agricultural workers. Climate change has also reduced Yemen's water resources and affected its coastal areas. In 2008 Yemen's Climate Change Unit at the General Authority of Environment Preservation warned that the continued effects of climate change could even lead to a "catastrophic drought."

Another example of climate change in Yemen can be seen by the increase in average temperatures in Sana'a during the past 20 years. There are fears that climate change will cause coastal flooding and that some of the main cities, including the important port of Hodeida, will eventually sink. The Ministry of Water and Environment is working with international experts to meet the many challenges posed by climate change. It is also following the United Nations Framework Convention on Climate Change. A March 2008 UN Food and Agriculture Organization (FAO) report on the Near East found Yemen to be at particularly high risk of a severe food crisis and widespread hunger because of its "existing low income levels, rapidly growing population, and acute water shortage."

NATURAL CATASTROPHES

In recent years Yemen has suffered from a number of natural disasters. This region of Arabia is prone to natural catastrophes, as it lies along the Rift Valley, which consists of a series of moving tectonic plates. There was an earthquake on December 13, 1982, in northern Yemen, which resulted in around 3,000 deaths and extensive damage.

A devastating landslide occurred in the village of al-Dhafeer, located around 31 miles (50 km) west of Sana'a, on December 28, 2005, destroying 20 homes and killing more than 90 people.

A volcano erupted on September 30, 2007, on an island off the coast of Yemen. On this occasion, the death rate was low, as the island does not have any permanent residents. Unfortunately a military base was situated there, and a few soldiers lost their lives.

One of the most recent disasters was the flooding during October 2008. It caused 180 deaths and millions of dollars in damage. The worst affected areas were in Hadramawt, Lahij, al-Mahrah, and Ta'izz, with most of the fatalities in Hadramawt. Homes, schools, and businesses were destroyed, as were essential infrastructure and farmland.

Houses and other buildings destroyed by torrential rains and floods in southeastern Yemen.

POLLUTION

Air pollution in Yemen is caused by a variety of factors, including emissions from vehicles and the widespread use of heavy construction tools such as industrial saws. The main source of air pollution, however, particularly in cities such as Sana'a, is emissions from cars and other vehicles. In Sana'a alone, there are about 250,000 vehicles, many of which are very old, having been brought into the country by returning Yemenis after the Gulf War in 1990. The majority of these vehicles use leaded gasoline or local diesel, which contains a high level of impurities. In fact, Yemen remains one of the few countries worldwide that continues to use leaded gasoline in its cars and other vehicles.

Air pollution is unpleasant and unhealthy. Breathing highly polluted air from exhaust fumes on a daily basis can cause severe respiratory and renal problems as well as other ailments such as ophthalmia. Air pollution represents a financial and environmental burden on the Yemeni government. In 2008, Yemen's Ministry of Water and Environment (MWE) acknowledged the severity of the problem, and it is working on a national strategy to reduce air pollution. The authorities have already implemented a few simple measures to improve the air quality. For example, vehicles that were manufactured

The proper handling of garbage is sometimes a problem in Yemen.

A YEMENI OIL SPILL

In 2002 an oil tanker exploded off the coast of Yemen. Approximately 700 tons (635,029 kg), or 5,000 barrels, of oil from one of its cargo tanks spilled into the sea. The type of oil being carried by this particular tanker was a heavy viscous Arabian crude oil. Its consistency made the cleanup operation along the shoreline more challenging. Cleaning the oil spill involved a great deal of manual labor, with workers having to shovel the oil into bags that they then carried away from the affected areas. Marine life along this shoreline was affected, with many birds becoming covered in oil.

before the year 2000 are no longer permitted entry into the country. The authorities have also reduced the tax on new cars to encourage more people to invest in newly built, modern, and more environmentally friendly vehicles.

Another source of pollution in Yemen, particularly around its coastal areas, is the oil industry. Although oil accounts for a large part of Yemen's revenue and is an invaluable economic resource, its production, exploration, and transportation have contributed significantly to coastal and maritime pollution in the Red Sea and the Gulf of Aden.

A survey conducted in 1989 by the Department of Oceanography at the Faculty of Science in Alexandria, Egypt, revealed that the Red Sea received an estimated 33 pounds of oil input per year for every square mile (15 kg of oil for every square km), while other bodies of water received an average of 20 pounds (9 kg).

The oil industry isn't responsible for all the pollution of Yemen's marine environment. Urbanization, the rapid development of coastal areas, and recreation and tourism contribute to the pollution levels as well. Desalination plants, water-treatment facilities, coastal mining, and quarrying are also responsible for the worsening pollution problems within the marine environment and along the coasts of Yemen.

Yet another cause of marine pollution comes from the increasing use of chemicals in certain agricultural activities. The fertilizers, pesticides, and insecticides used extensively in modern farming end up flowing toward and into the sea and coastal areas, causing damage to the marine life and the surrounding environment.

YEMENIS

A Yemeni man in his traditional outfit and dagger.

CHAPTER 6

THE MAJORITY OF YEMENIS are Arabs—people who originate from the Arabian Peninsula and surrounding territories and whose mother tongue is Arabic. Although many Yemenis speak the same language, there is an extraordinary diversity among them.

There are variations in religious affiliation among regions, among tribes, and within society. Underneath those differences, though, the Yemeni people are straightforward, kind, full of life, and down-to-earth.

The creativity and skilled craftsmanship of the Yemeni Jews had a major impact on the indigenous non-Jewish culture. When the Jews departed, many traditional crafts disappeared.

Local boys sitting by a wadi in Yemen.

POPULATION

With a population of more than 23 million, Yemen is one of the most densely populated areas in the Arabian Peninsula. In comparison, neighboring Oman has a population of only 3.4 million. Saudi Arabia has a population of 28 million, but its land area is four times the size of Yemen. The average population density in Yemen is 116 people per square mile (45 people per square km). The majority of Yemenis live in small villages scattered across the countryside. About 28 percent live in cities or towns, and this percentage is increasing as the country develops. Urban growth stood at 4.6 percent in 2008. Around 46 percent of the population is below the age of 14.

The population is growing fast, at an annual rate of 3.5 percent, as the average woman bears about six babies during her lifetime. In the early 1990s, when the men returned from the Gulf Region, the population peaked.

Local children posing for a photograph. There are many young people in Yemen. More than half of the population is under 15 years old.

THE ARABS

The majority of Yemenis are Arabs, but they divide themselves into two groups based on their genealogy. The first group, the southern Arabs, are sons of Qahtan and originated in Yemen. Qahtan was the son of Shem and the grandson of Noah. The Hashid and Bakil tribal groups trace their ancestry from Qahtan and are said to be related to the ancient Sabeans. The second group, the northern Arabs, are the sons of Adnan. Adnan is the Islamic version of the biblical Ishmael, one of Abraham's sons. Sayyids, who are members of Yemen's religious elite, are northern Arabs. Historians confirm that both groups have been in Arabia from the earliest known times.

Yemeni Jews walking in the desert.

Throughout most of their history, the Arabs of the interior have not been exposed to intruders, because the desert and the sea kept out foreign influences. There is more racial mixing in the towns and the seaports. For example, some of the people living along the Red Sea are of African descent.

YEMENI JEWS

The number of Jews in Yemen is certainly not reflective of their importance. For centuries, the Jews were the largest non-Muslim group living permanently in Yemen. Most of them were descendants of the indigenous people who adopted Judaism in pre-Islamic times. When the State of Israel was founded in 1948, the Jews left Yemen in droves. Almost half of the population in Sana'a used to be Jewish. Today there are just a few thousand in the whole country, mainly elderly and living in mountain villages.

The Western perception, largely influenced by Hollywood, of the traditional Arab is of the bedouin—camel-breeding tribes who roam the deserts. But the majority of the tribes in Yemen are not nomadic; they are sedentary cultivators. Only about 1 percent of the population are bedouin, and they are concentrated in the eastern governorates, especially al-Mahrah. Of course, this is just an estimate, since it is difficult to get an accurate census of nomads.

The bedouin have always been fiercely proud of their freedom and ability to survive with the bare necessities: their livestock, a tent, a rug, and a few cooking pots. Despite their remarkable independence, they have never lived in total isolation. Throughout history they have sold their thoroughbred camels to villagers and townspeople and have purchased items that they could not produce themselves, including a few luxuries such as tobacco.

Today many bedouin have settled or gone to work in the oil fields. Others still lead a more traditional lifestyle, but the tracks of four-wheel-drive vehicles that cut through the desert are telltale signs of change.

Under the Zaidi imams, the Jews were a protected group. Although there were restrictions on their lives, they were accepted as part of the social order. Many were employed as merchants, moneychangers, and craftsmen. The beautifully handcrafted Yemeni silverware best displays their creative talents.

Many Yemeni Jews are known for being religious and having a great amount of knowledge about Jewish religious practices. In fact members of the Yemeni Jewish community are known to be able to conduct synagogue

Male villagers stand united with their sons in front of their village.

services themselves instead of relying on the services of a rabbi. As religion plays such an important role in many Yemeni Jewish communities, the synagogue is the focus for religious as well as social life. Families come together regularly to meet and maintain their traditions and customs. All types of celebrations and rituals—marriages, births, funerals—are marked with traditional customs involving food, music, poetry, and dance.

A Yemeni Jewish custom that is still practiced today is the *h'inna* party, which is essentially a celebration that takes place before a wedding where the bride-to-be is honored by being dressed up in elaborate costumes and traditional jewelry. Friends and family gather around her singing celebratory songs, playing music, and dancing.

SOCIAL STRUCTURE

Yemenis have traditionally been stratified by descent, distinguishing those of religious status from the tribal farmers and those who worked in the marketplace. In theory these status distinctions are a relic of the past, but nevertheless they still exist.

In the Hadramawt region, women working in the fields wear long, black robes and straw hats to protect themselves from the blazing sun.

At the apex of the social pyramid are the sayyids, who are descendants of the prophet Muhammad. During the Zaidi imamate, they held important government positions and were wealthy landlords. Because of their education, religious knowledge, and administrative expertise, sayyids are respected to this day. Quite a number of them are teachers, healers, and mediators in tribal disputes. Another elite group are the *qadis*, Islamic scholars of law. Their status is also hereditary, and a number of great qadi families have played important roles in Yemen's history, such as Abdul Rahman al-Iryani, president of the former Yemen Arab Republic.

Tribal people of Qahtani ancestry fall below the elite groups in terms of social status and are farmers. Each tribal unit is headed by a sheikh, who is a wise man of good character. He oversees village affairs and may sometimes act as a government official. The members of a tribe have a strong sense of belonging, and each tribe has its own characteristic dress, poetry, dance, and cuisine.

Below the tribal people are those members of society of unrecognized descent. These people perform various services—they may be butchers, barbers, or wedding musicians. At the bottom of the social pyramid are those who perform menial jobs such as sweeping the streets. In the past, these people were social outcasts.

People's attitudes have been changing in recent years, and as a result, the traditional social hierarchy is weakening. With the emergence of a market economy, the menial occupations formerly given low status have become more respected. In addition, education is no longer confined to the elite members of society. Therefore literacy is slowly spreading among those near the bottom of the social pyramid.

RURAL/URBAN DIVISIONS

As in many other countries all over the world, in Yemen the division between the rural and the urban populations is as important as social distinctions. The tribal people are rural folk who work in the agricultural sector, while the sayyids, the qadis, and those employed in trade, commerce, or manufacturing industries perceive themselves as city folk.

There is a bit of good-natured competition between the urban and the rural people. The tribal people consider city folk to be weaker and less healthy, and some city folk consider the rural people to be less sophisticated. But these differences will become less pronounced as mobility increases.

MEN'S WEAR

The saying "you are what you wear" is certainly descriptive of traditional male attire. Clothing identifies where a man comes from, his tribe, and his position in society. The type of headgear and the way it is worn and the appearance and position of his dagger are important too.

Traditional male tribal dress consists of a *futa* (FOO-ta), which is a wraparound skirt; a handwoven turban; and a *jambiya* (JAHM-bi-yah), which is a ceremonial dagger. The dagger is worn upright and centered and is kept in place by a leather or cloth belt. You can tell the status of a man by the design and the materials used to make his dagger. You can tell which tribe a man belongs to by the way he wraps his turban around his head. In addition, he might wear a short coat made of woven wool or sheepskin. A shawl thrown over the shoulders serves to keep him warm and can also be used as a handy tote bag.

Today dress patterns are changing. In the cities more men are wearing suits, ties, and other forms of Western-style clothing. Traditional clothing is often combined with Western-style shirts and blazers, and colorful imported cloth covers the head. Many Yemeni men, both in the cities and in rural areas, wear more traditional Arab clothing that consists of cotton breeches or a striped kilt. Many men wear skullcaps, turbans, or tall, round hats called tarbooshes. Tribal dress has also become fashionable among nontribesmen.

A man adorns himself with a rifle and a *jambiya*. These weapons are carried more as status symbols than for self-defense in Yemen. Yemeni men's headgear, like the rest of the clothing, identifies their clan loyalties.

WOMEN'S WEAR

In Yemen women tend to dress to reflect their regional and social status. The regional variation in clothing styles among Yemeni women is fantastic; rural and urban women dress quite differently.

Many Yemeni women wear loose long tunics or dresses, and the majority cover their heads with shawls and veils. Most women wear leg coverings such as bloomers, slacks, or dark tights under their dresses or tunics.

In many urban and even in some rural areas, women have adopted Western dress. At home younger women wear jeans, T-shirts, and sweaters. For special occasions such as religious festivals or weddings, women wear their loveliest outfits and traditional jewelry. Glittering silver adorns the neck, the ankles, the wrists, and sometimes the forehead.

In accordance with Islamic rules, many Yemeni women cover themselves with veils and robes.

As Yemen is a Muslim country, the women dress modestly and tend to veil themselves in the presence of strange men. The veiling of women is not a law in Yemen as it is in Saudi Arabia. Some younger, educated women in urban areas cover their heads but not their faces. In fact there are a few women who choose not to wear a veil at all. For a brief period in socialist South Yemen, urban women chose to adopt a Western style of dress and rejected the veil. Since unification, however, the majority of women in Yemen today wear a form of head covering in response to a growing conservatism. Women who choose to wear a veil in Yemen do so because of tradition, not because they are required to.

The outer head coverings among urban and rural women are different. Rural women may wear one or more scarves on their head and a woolen shawl for weddings or when traveling beyond their village. These shawls are placed on the head in a variety of interesting ways and can enhance their femininity. Rural women frequently wear a broad-brimmed straw hat called a *dhola* (DOH-ler) to protect themselves from the sun while working outdoors.

BODY PAINTING

Despite the influx of European cosmetics, women and girls still paint themselves with traditional makeup for special occasions. Before a religious festival, women will paint black floral designs on their hands and feet with a substance called khidab *(KEY-dab).*

In Sana'a it is customary for a bride to be embellished by an experienced body painter before her wedding. The ink is applied to the body with a needle, an acacia thorn, or even a toothpick. The face and the neck are decorated, as are the arms from the hands to the shoulders and the legs from the feet to the knees. Although there are catalogs containing various patterns, an experienced body painter uses her imagination to create vivid designs. This ritual takes several hours and a lot of patience!

In the Tihama, many women are not veiled. They wear hats woven from palm fronds, resembling those worn in Mexico. Women in the mountains drape sprigs of sweet-smelling basil over their ears for decoration or to protect against the evil eye or evil spirits.

Most urban women wear a face veil and are frequently enveloped in a *sharshaf* (SHAHR-shahf), which is a loose, black garment that covers the body, or are gracefully attired in a *sitara* (SEE-tahr-a), a brightly colored covering. Another common form of covering is the abaya, a loose black robe that covers the women from head to toe and is also worn by women in many other Arab countries. Professional urban women wear a headscarf and a coat. The hijab, a headscarf that covers the hair and the neck, is also popular.

The colors that the women wear are different from region to region. In Sana'a many women wear bright cloths imported from India. Women in the Tihama region dress in colorful garments, and in eastern Yemen women working in the fields wear black robes.

LIFESTYLE

Locals enjoying a typical day in a market.

CHAPTER 7

YEMENI FARMERS, herders, fishermen, and professionals all lead very different lives. In the rural parts, daily life is physically strenuous. In the city, amid the hustle and bustle, people from all kinds of backgrounds intermingle. In spite of their differences, though, a similar set of values regulates the lives of both city and rural dwellers: Living in a group (be it family, tribe, or village) is more important than living alone.

Like people in many other developing countries with more conservative values, Yemenis, in particular the young, are increasingly exposed to foreign influences such as nightclubs and pop music. Modern influences from television and other media mainly come from neighboring countries such as Syria and Egypt.

Motorcycles are very highly prized in Yemen. These nifty vehicles make traveling through the narrow streets and enclaves much easier.

SOCIAL VALUES

Friends often gather for food, either at a restaurant or at a person's home. Such socialization is an intricate part of Yemeni life.

Yemenis place great value on family ties. Most responsibilities are shared among relatives, friends, and neighbors. When someone goes on a trip, a neighbor might take care of essential tasks such as tending the livestock. If anyone is missing from a gathering, a friend or a neighbor will drop by to ensure that everything is all right. When two people are arguing in the street, a bystander may step in to mediate.

Yemenis are well known for their politeness, hospitality, and generosity, especially toward guests and those less fortunate. Perhaps the queen of Sheba started the tradition of hospitality when she showered King Solomon with gifts.

A guest is honored and welcomed as though part of the family. The host will do just about anything to ensure that visitors feel at home, plying them with plenty of food, drink, gifts, and entertainment. This warm-hearted generosity is not confined to the home. For example, when a Yemeni is eating in front of another, he or she will always offer to share the food.

THE PACE OF LIFE

Human relationships are extremely important in Yemen. Whether in a mountain village or in the city, people always have time to exchange a smile and a greeting. People in the villages live in close proximity, especially in the mountains, where the houses are huddled together. There is plenty of social interaction, as daily chores are rarely performed in isolation; there is always time to chat with one's neighbors.

In the cities life is faster, more cosmopolitan, and less personal. Yet people still approach their work differently than most urban Westerners do. When conducting business, some time is always devoted to exchanging family news, and the common phrase *insha' Allah* (EEN-sha Allah), which means "God willing," reveals the Yemeni attitude that time and deadlines are flexible. Being friendly and polite are important attributes when conducting business and getting things done successfully in Yemen. In both the cities and the countryside, men and women get together (in separate groups) in the afternoons to sip tea, chew khat, and chat. A number of city offices close for these afternoon gatherings.

A typical family unit in Yemen.

THE FAMILY

A Yemeni family may consist of a whole collection of relatives who live under the same roof. Very few people in Yemen live on their own. Grandparents, widows, and divorcees are all taken under the family wing. However, the number of family members living under the same roof is decreasing. Some men move into their own house when they marry. This gives the new wife more freedom to run her own household.

There is a prescribed order regulating family life. Each family member has a specific role and responsibility based on his or her age and sex. For both men and women, authority is based on seniority. The elderly command the utmost respect, and their opinions are highly valued. They are often asked to mediate in disputes.

A proud mother shows off her child. Yemeni parents love their children dearly, and large families are common.

Traditionally the head of the household is the father, who provides for his family, although the mother plays an important role. She raises the children and takes care of the household chores, although she may not be confined to this role.

In more patriarchal families the men generally assume tasks that require contact with the public, such as shopping in the market for household provisions. Women cook, clean, and do the washing. Younger and fitter women also do the more strenuous work, such as carrying water and fetching fuel. In urban areas the traditional roles within a family are changing as more women now go to work.

CHILDREN

To the Yemenis, children are gifts from God and welcomed after marriage. Due to limited hospital facilities, many women deliver babies at home, assisted by an older female family member or a midwife.

A large family is highly valued in rural areas because there will be more people to help with the many chores. Children have to help look after their younger siblings and harvest the crops. These days, however, it is harder to make a living from the land, so more women choose to have smaller families so that they can afford to educate their children for nonagricultural jobs.

Yemeni parents are proud of their children and raise them in a loving environment. Girls are taught to be patient, loving, modest, and helpful. Boys learn that they must protect the women of their family and uphold the family honor. The children also pick up other skills required for an urban or a rural life from their parents, grandparents, and older brothers and sisters. In cities boys may learn how to conduct a business deal or ride a motorcycle, while girls may learn how to operate modern cooking appliances. In rural areas boys may learn how to operate or repair a diesel pump, while girls learn how to sew and cook.

ARRANGED MARRIAGES

Most marriages are arranged by the families of the prospective couple, but they are rarely forced. Family members play an important part in matchmaking and bringing together suitable couples. For example, in a small town, a young man might know a girl by sight, but he would have few chances of meeting her, as there is a greater segregation of the sexes than in Western countries. Therefore he would have to rely on the advice of his mother or sister, who would know the women of the neighborhood well.

A mother plays a significant part in choosing a suitable wife for her son. sIn more traditional communities, once she has decided on a girl, normally based on her dignity and status, a mother confers with her husband. If both parents agree on the choice, they consult their son. After a prospective wife has been chosen, father and son pay a visit to the house of the bride's family to speak to her father. However, the decision is not made right away. The potential father-in-law has to think it over and discuss the matter with his daughter. Only when everybody agrees is a date fixed for the betrothal.

The betrothal is quite an informal affair. Father and son, along with a few male relatives, deliver a number of gifts, such as raisins, dates, clothes, and khat, to the bride's house. They also give the engagement ring to the girl's father for safekeeping. Then they discuss suitable dates for the wedding and agree on a bride price, which is usually paid in cash. At this point, the couple are officially engaged, and the wedding plans begin.

Once the couple are married, their families continue to play an important role in supporting their marriage.

EDUCATION

Until the 1960s formal education was primarily the privilege of the elite members of society. Many children were schooled in the village mosque, where instruction was oral and the emphasis was on memorizing the Koran rather than learning to read and write. A lucky few went to Aden or Egypt to be educated, but many children remained illiterate. In addition getting to school is more difficult for children who live in remote rural areas than for those in urban centers, because of inadequate transportation.

Today everyone has the right to an elementary education, which is free and compulsory. Children start elementary school at six years of age and finish at 15. After this, some children continue their studies in secondary school until the age of 18. In Yemen today males receive an average of 11 years of education, while females receive an average of seven years.

More Yemeni children are able to read and write than before, but there is still a gap in literacy between girls and boys. In fact the issue of girls' education is a problem that Yemen continues to address. School enrollment and retention rates for girls are low compared with those for boys. The illiteracy rate for females stands at 76 percent in Yemen. For the minority who pursue higher education, there are modern universities and a number of vocational training centers. At the university in Sana'a, students can choose from a number of degree programs: arts, science, medicine, law, commerce, and education. The extended family comes in handy for young mothers, enabling them to continue their studies, as everybody pitches in to look after the children.

In 2006 schools in the cities of Sana'a, Aden, al-Mukalla, and Ta'izz participated in Internet for Yemeni High Schools, an initiative organized by the Society for Women and Children and the Education Development Center (EDC). The aim was to connect high schools in Yemen with those in the United States by developing an online learning network. The project was a success and provided improved information and communication technology (ICT) access for students in Yemen, who were previously not able to access it. In 2007 the Yemen Ministry of Education, with support from the United States Agency for International Development, the Middle East Partnership Initiative, and the EDC, organized a summit to examine new methods of teaching and learning in Yemeni schools. As a result of these types of initiatives, a growing number of schools in Yemen today are using ICT applications such as multimedia CD-ROMs, digital video, radio, computers, and the Internet.

Until the early 1990s, only a quarter of all females in Yemen attended school. After unification, a new constitution was passed stating the right of all citizens to an education. More girls now have the opportunity to pursue higher education.

Yemenis were already inoculating themselves with the blood of small-pox survivors long before Western-ers developed this technique.

HEALTH

According to the World Health Organization's 2006 figures, Yemen's expenditure on health as a percentage of its GDP stands at 4.6 percent. Yemen's life expectancy is 59 years for males and 62 years for females. The United States, in comparison, spends 15.3 percent of its GDP on health, and life expectancy is 75 years for males and 80 years for females.

Modern health services are being developed in Yemen, but there are still not enough doctors or hospital beds. One obstacle to providing proper health facilities is that many people are scattered in small villages. The shortage of drinking water and poor sanitation contribute to diseases such as tuberculosis and typhoid.

Yemen has a long tradition of folk medicine. There are healers throughout the country with their own special herbal remedies to cure ailments and diseases. A well-known folk remedy is barberry, used to alleviate internal bleeding and stomach problems. Sadly some of this folk wisdom is not being passed on, nor is it being incorporated into modern medical practices.

Some Yemenis believe that there are evil or mischievous forces that can cause sickness. Charms, amulets, and plants are used to control these forces. One important plant is rue, an evergreen shrub. The leaves of the rue are worn to ward off the evil eye. Words are also thought to be curative, and it is not uncommon for Koranic verses to be recited over a sick person.

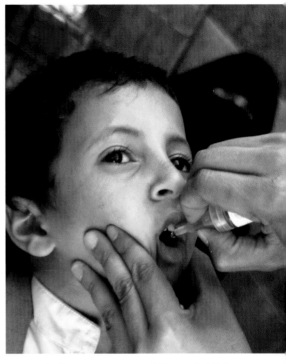

A Yemeni child receives a polio vaccine during a three-day immunization campaign at a health center in Sana'a, Yemen launched the campaign targeting more than 4.2 million children under five years of age due to the spread of polio in a number of neighboring countries.

INSIDE A TOWER HOUSE

A tower house is a multistory house with many attractively decorated rooms. Each family unit has its own room or story, while certain communal areas are shared. The ground floor is usually used for storage. Families live on the upper stories, where there are bedrooms, sitting rooms, dining areas, kitchens, and bathrooms.

ANCIENT MEDICINE

There is an ancient body of medical literature in Yemen. Some of this knowledge is based on the findings of the ancient Egyptians and Greeks. The Greeks believed that the human body consisted of four elements: earth, fire, air, and water. The combination of these elements in a person's body was supposed to give them a particular "temperament," and one had to balance these elements in order to stay healthy.

A distinctive Islamic medical tradition grew out of these principles and built on the practices of the prophet Muhammad and his companions regarding health and sickness. These practices stressed the importance of fresh air, exercise, and diet. The Rasulids, who ruled from the 13th to 15th centuries, developed sophisticated medical literature on herbs, surgery, diseases, magical treatments, and preventative diet. The importance of eating different foods during different months and seasons was emphasized. Hot, fatty foods were to be eaten in October, for example, while cold, wet foods such as fish and sour milk were recommended for June.

People often sleep in different rooms depending on the season, occupying the warmest ones in winter. Old people are given light and airy rooms to make them more comfortable. The rooms are usually furnished similarly, with a chest or a trunk for a person's personal items and some wooden pegs for hanging clothes.

The interior of a traditional house in Zabid.

The best room in the house, the *mafraj* (MAHF-rahj), is also the highest. It is therefore perfect for enjoying a view of Yemen's dreamy landscapes. The walls are often whitewashed and decorated with delicate patterns and verses of poetry. The floor may be covered with mattresses, carpets, and decorative cushions. This is where socializing, entertaining, and other leisure activities take place. Afternoons are spent here eating snacks, chewing khat, listening to music, and exchanging the latest news.

Male strangers are supposed to stay out of the areas used by women. If they have to pass the women's quarters on the way to the *mafraj*, they call out "Allah Allah" to announce their approach, so that the women can shut their doors or cover their faces.

Building techniques for these distinctive tower houses have been passed down from generation to generation. Many Arabic houses are built around a secluded courtyard. Yemeni houses, however, are usually built to face outward, often overlooking a public space or street. The exterior walls of many of these tower houses have been exquisitely decorated with ancient motifs including Sabean script, intricate geometric patterns, and ancient symbols of snakes and water. The windows of these tower houses come in different shapes and sizes—rectangles, circles, and semicircles. They are often beautifully decorated with stained glass.

A traditional tower house in Yemen.

RELIGION

An evening view of the new mosque in Sana'a.

CHAPTER 8

ISLAM WAS BORN IN THE same geographic area as Christianity and Judaism. The followers of all three faiths share the same God, the main difference being their understanding of his prophets or messengers.

There are various Islamic schools of thought, and different Muslim communities follow their own interpretation of the Koran. For instance Shiism and Sunnism are divisions within Islam. The majority of Yemenis practice Islam as a religion and a way of life. Islam is the official religion, but there is a small number of Christians and Jews.

THE PROPHET

Muhammad was born in Mecca, an important trading and cultural center in Saudi Arabia, in A.D. 570. Even as a boy, Muhammad disliked the beliefs of his fellow Arabs. When he was older, he became a traveling merchant. He was successful, but disturbed by the greed around him, he often retreated to the mountains to think. At the age of 25 he married a noblewoman, Khadija, and they had six children.

When Muhammad was 40, a profound experience changed his life. According to Islamic tradition, the angel Gabriel appeared to Muhammad one night, and for more than 20 years thereafter communicated God's words to him. These revelations concerned issues of religion, government, human conduct, and relationships.

Encouraged by his wife, Muhammad began preaching to the people of Mecca, urging them to abandon the idols they worshiped and lead better lives. The city's establishment first became concerned, then

Allah has what is known as 99 names or attributes, including the Gracious, the Merciful, the Compassionate, the Kind, the All-Knowing, the All-Wise, the Lord of the Universe, and the Creator.

hostile as Muhammad's following grew. Muhammad and his followers fled north to Medina in A.D. 622. This became known as the Hegira, or the year of migration, and is year one of the Islamic calendar.

In Medina the Muslim community continued to grow stronger. By A.D. 630 Muslims had conquered Mecca. Today Muslims are found all over the world. They may be Arabs, Indonesians, Indians, Africans, Americans, or other nationalities.

SUNNISM AND SHIISM

When Muhammad died in A.D. 632, one of his close friends, Abu Bakr, was chosen to lead the Muslim community. Sometime after Abu Bakr's death, when a group called the Shia refused to accept one of the later successors, a major split developed within Islam. The division between Shiism and Sunnism remains to this day. The Shias believe that Muslim leadership should be descended from Ali, Muhammad's cousin and son-in-law, because they consider Ali to be the first spiritual leader. The Sunnis, who are considered to be more traditional and orthodox, believe that elected members of the Muslim community can become leaders. Both divisions agree on most of the major matters of faith and worship, but some of their laws are different.

This man belongs to the Ismaili sect of Shiism, which expanded into Yemen from eastern Arabia and Egypt in the year 1061.

Within Shiism and Sunnism, there are different sects. About 42 percent of Yemen's population are Zaidis, a Shia sect. The Ismailis, another Shia sect, make up about 1 percent of the population. About 55 percent of the population are Sunni Muslims who belong to the Shafi'i sect.

THE KORAN, THE SUNNA, AND THE HADITH

The Islamic faith is based on the Koran, a book of God's words spoken through the prophet Muhammad. Muslims accept the Bible but believe that the Koran is the supreme source of divine instruction.

The Koran is divided into 114 suras, or chapters, which have multiple verses. Muslims try to memorize as many verses as they can.

Muslims believe that the life of Muhammad embodied the teachings of the Koran and is therefore another source of guidance. Many of his sayings were memorized and preserved by his companions. The Hadith is a collection of these sayings. It instructs Muslims on daily activities, such as washing before praying. The Sunna refers to the way of life prescribed for Muslims on the basis of the teachings and practices of Muhammad and interpretations of the Koran.

THE FIVE PILLARS OF ISLAM

Besides accepting Islam's beliefs, a Muslim must fulfill a list of religious duties. These duties play an important part in maintaining a sense of belonging to the Muslim community. They are commonly known as the Five Pillars of Islam.

1. SHAHADAH (sha-HAHD-a) is confession and the essence of a Muslim's faith. It involves reciting two statements: "There is no God but God" and "Muhammad is the prophet of God." Muslims repeat these statements daily in prayer. The belief that Muhammad is God's ultimate messenger is a key element distinguishing Islam from Judaism and Christianity.

2. SALAT (sa-LAHT) is prayer. A Muslim must pray five times a day, at sunrise, midday, midafternoon, sunset, and night. Prayers can be performed anywhere—at school, at work, at home, outdoors—but there is a prescribed form. Before praying, Muslims must be in a state of mental and physical purity. They first gargle and spit to cleanse their mouth. Then they wash their face, neck, hands, arms, and feet.

Praying involves reciting parts of the Koran, bowing, kneeling, and touching the head to the ground, symbolizing submission to God. Some Muslims kneel on a prayer rug as they pray. While praying, Muslims face the direction of Mecca, the spiritual center of Islam. Mecca is where the central shrine of pilgrimage for Muslims, called the Kaaba, lies. The Kaaba is a small stone building that houses the Black Stone. Muslims believe that this stone fell from paradise when Adam and Eve were cast out.

According to Islamic tradition, all Muslims should give alms before the end of Ramadan. Almsgiving is supposed to purify the giver's soul.

PURIFICATION

A fundamental requirement of Islam is ritual purity. A prayer has no value unless one has purified oneself in mind and body beforehand. According to the Koran, water is the beginning of life and should be used for purifying the body. Wherever there is water, there is usually a place of prayer. In the highlands of Yemen, worshipers gather around streams and ponds to  *make their ablutions and pray. In the cities worshipers frequently purify themselves in bathhouses. Almost every mosque has an ablution pool. Throughout the Arabian Peninsula, however, water is not always easy to come by. In such cases, the worshiper can make the ablution with sand or simply go through the motions with the hands.*

3. ZAKAT (za-KAHT) is almsgiving. According to the Koran, one is supposed to give up one's "surplus." So the third pillar involves giving a certain percentage of one's wealth to the poor and needy.

4. SAWM (sa-AHM) is fasting. All Muslims are expected to go without food or drink during the daylight hours of the month of Ramadan. Everyone is required to fast except small children, the elderly, nursing mothers, and the infirm. Those traveling may refrain from fasting, but they must make up the days at a later date. Life slows nearly to a standstill during Ramadan, and many shops stay closed until after the midday prayers. Muslims believe that during Ramadan, the gates of paradise are opened and the gates of hell are closed, and the sins of those who fast will be forgiven. This is a time of religious contemplation. Muslims stay up late at night to read the Koran, and they visit the mosque more often than usual. At the end of the month there is a great festival with rich food and presents. This is known as Eid al-Fitr, a celebration of the breaking of the fast.

RITES OF THE HAJJ

The hajj is not just a trip to Mecca. Numerous rituals must be performed, and Muslims prepare themselves by studying these under a religious leader. At a certain point on the road to Mecca, pilgrims must purify themselves, don the hajj garments, and proclaim their intention to make the pilgrimage. Upon arrival, they pray at the Great Mosque and walk around the Kaaba seven times, touching or kissing the Black Stone. Afterward they visit other holy sites in the vicinity.

Some of the other rites include running between the hills of Safa and Marwa; drinking from the well of Zamzam to commemorate the desperate search of Hajira, one of the prophet Ibrahim's wives, for water for her baby; and standing for most of the day in meditation at Mount Arafat, where Muhammad gave a famous sermon. On the way back to Mecca, Muslims stop at Mina to perform another symbolic act known as stoning the devil. Small stones about the size of peas are thrown at pillars that represent the temptations of Satan.

The pilgrimage concludes with the sacrifice of an animal, usually a sheep, a goat, or a camel. To signify the successful completion of the hajj, the ritual ablution involves snipping a few locks of hair and trimming the nails.

In the past, the muezzin called Muslims to prayer from the top of a minaret. Today, the call is usually recorded and broadcast over loudspeakers.

5. HAJJ (HAHJ) is pilgrimage to Mecca. At least once in a lifetime, Muslims who can afford it should travel to the holy city of Mecca. The pilgrimage represents an act of obedience to God and should be made in the 12th and last month of the Islamic year. Eid al-Adha, or the Feast of the Sacrifice, marks the last day of the pilgrimage, which lasts 10 days.

Each year millions of Muslims from all over the world travel to Mecca. The pilgrims wear simple white robes that make it impossible to distinguish the rich from the poor. They are symbolic of the Islamic belief that all men are equal before God. Pilgrims do not wear perfume or jewelry. They must abandon any vanity and seek forgiveness, guidance, and salvation from God.

THE MOSQUE

When Muhammad and his followers arrived in Medina in A.D. 622, there was no suitable place where they could worship. Therefore they gathered in Muhammad's house to listen to his sermons and to pray. His house became known as a *masjid* (MAHS-jid), which is Arabic for "mosque." This is a place of prayer and worship, as well as a place of rest and study.

Traditional mosques are rectangular and built of brick or stone or whatever material is locally available. There is a slender tower from which the muezzin, or mosque official, gives the call for Muslims to pray.

Mosques have similar features. There is a courtyard with a place for worshipers to wash and leave their shoes. Inside the prayer hall is a special niche in one wall indicating the direction of Mecca. There is also a pulpit for the prayer leader. The prayer hall is a single large room with carpets for worshipers to kneel on. There are usually other rooms for study groups.

Many mosques are richly decorated with geometric designs and verses from the Koran. In most mosques there are no religious scenes of God or Muhammad, as the majority of Muslim communities forbid the use of graven images.

PRAYER AND DAILY LIFE

Muslims divide their day according to the five obligatory prayer times. At dawn, the muezzin makes the first call to prayer.

The first person to wake rouses the rest of the family. Once out of bed, the men, often clad in the same white robes they wear as nightshirts, will set off for the mosque. The women usually pray in the privacy of their home. After morning prayer the daily routine begins. Children get ready for school, the women begin the day's cooking, and the men (and if they have jobs outside the home, the women, too) get ready for work.

When the sun reaches its peak, the muezzin calls the faithful for the midday prayer. After prayer, family members meet for lunch and then return to their daily activities.

When the sun is at a 45-degree angle to the earth, it is time for the afternoon prayer. Some men resume their work after this, while others get together to chew khat and discuss the events of the day. The women also have gatherings where they exchange news. The sunset prayer signals that it is time for the women to return to their homes. After the sunset prayer, the family eats supper. There is a little time for homework, watching television, or listening to the radio until the evening prayer. Then it is time for bed.

LANGUAGE

A man browses through the shelves of books in a local Yemeni bookstore.

CHAPTER 9

ARABIC IS ONE OF THE MOST expressive languages in the world. The written word is beautiful, and the spoken word is musical. The Arabic language occupies a special place in the hearts of its speakers because it is the sacred language of the Koran. It is also a secular language used in everyday situations. Yemen is one of many nations using Arabic.

THE ARABIC LANGUAGE

Broadly speaking, Arabic belongs to the Hamito-Semitic family of languages. More specifically, Arabic belongs to the Semitic group of languages and is closely related to Hebrew, the language of the Jews. Semitic people are descendants of Shem, the son of Noah. Arabic was first spoken 2,000 years ago by the people living on the Arabian Peninsula.

Nobody is quite sure how the language developed, but the Arabs have a myth about its origins. According to tradition, God put the Arabic language in Adam's mouth at the time of the Creation. When Adam disobeyed God, he was forbidden to speak Arabic and had to learn Syriac instead.

These Himyaritic writings were engraved on the stone of the old Ma'rib Dam in 600 B.C.

With the expansion of Islam, the Arabic language spread to other parts of the world. From its birthplace on the Arabian Peninsula, Islam spread east and west from the early seventh through the early 10th centuries. At its zenith, the Islamic empire and the use of the Arabic language extended from Spain across North Africa and through the Middle East to Central Asia and India. Today more than 225 million people speak Arabic. It is the official language of many countries in North Africa and the Middle East.

LETTERS AND NUMBERS

There is a great deal of discussion as to when the Arabic alphabet was invented. Some believe it was probably in the fourth century A.D., while others believe it was earlier. It has 28 characters and is written and read from right to left. There are no capital letters, but the shape of a letter changes depending on its position in a word. Arabic script has a rich variety of forms and makes for magnificent calligraphic decoration. The ancient Kufic script, which is heavy and angular, was used in the earliest copies of the Koran.

The Arabic script.

Many English words come from Arabic, including *alcohol*, *algebra*, *checkmate*, *lute*, *magazine*, and *zero*. Nevertheless, writing Arabic words into English is complicated. A few of the sounds used in Arabic have no equivalent in the English language, and most vowels are not written. Therefore an Arabic word can be rendered in English in a variety of ways. For example, both *Muslim* and *Moslem* are perfectly legitimate, as are *Muhammad*, *Mohammed*, and *Mehemet*.

Even the numbers that we use today come from the Arabs. Long ago the Christian world used Roman numerals, where letters represent numbers. For example, the letter *C* is 100, and the letter *M* is 1,000. Therefore, the figure 2,400 would appear as *MMCCCC*. The numbers *0, 1, 2, 3, 4, 5, 6, 7, 8,* and *9,* which are so familiar to us, are known as Arabic numerals. The symbols for all these digits, except zero, originated in India around 200 B.C. The zero was developed only after A.D. 600. The word *zero* is probably the Arabic version of the Hindu word *sunya*, which means "empty." Traders and merchants introduced this Arabic number system across the Mediterranean and into Spain. From Spain, it spread throughout Europe.

Arabic calligraphy carries with it years of Islamic history.

WRITING

The language used for writing throughout the Arab world is known as Classical Arabic. It is an ancient language, modeled after the language of the Koran. Classical Arabic has changed very little over the centuries.

Poets and writers used Classical Arabic in the early Islamic period. It is considered the most eloquent form of Arabic. All Muslims, regardless of their native tongue, perform their recitations in Classical Arabic because they believe that to translate the words of God from that sacred language would be impious.

Many alphabetic scripts used along the Mediterranean coastline are traceable to the Phoenician alphabet of about 1000 B.C. The Phoenician script was an advancement from the pictorial script used by the Egyptians. It was spread by Phoenician sailors and merchants who traded their goods with the peoples of the eastern Mediterranean. Hebrew and Aramaic evolved from Phoenician.

Although the history of writing is not entirely certain, it appears that two variations of the Phoenician script, known as the North and the South Arabian scripts, were in use on the Arabian Peninsula around 500 B.C. The South Arabian script was also called the Sabean script, named after the legendary kingdom of Saba. Thousands of Sabean inscriptions carved in stone or engraved on bronze statues have been discovered in many parts of southern Arabia. The Sabean script is also found in some of the earliest Ethiopian inscriptions. With the decline of the kingdom of Saba, the script fell into disuse, and the Arabic used today did not come from the Sabeans.

Classical Arabic is a difficult language to read, even for those who speak it. Moreover, it lacks many words necessary in today's world. As a result, a simplified version of Classical Arabic, known as Modern Standard Arabic, was developed in the last century. It is much easier to read and allows for the expression of modern concepts. Children in all Arab countries learn to read and write Modern Standard Arabic, and it is the language of radio, television, novels, films, and legal documents. Each Arabic-speaking country or region has its own form of spoken Arabic.

SPEAKING

Although Arabs share a common written language, variations in the spoken word have evolved over time. Today spoken Arabic, also known as Colloquial Arabic, consists of four dialects: Syrian, Arabian Peninsula, Moroccan, and Egyptian. Some of these are mutually unintelligible; although two literate Arabs can communicate by using Classical Arabic, most Yemenis would find it difficult to converse with a Moroccan. Local dialects also vary within a country. In Yemen certain Arabic letters are pronounced differently in the north than they are in the south.

Yemeni boys having a conversation.

The Arabic language is an emotional one and has a powerful effect on its users. This is evident when Arabs are reciting poetry, chanting the Koran, or giving a speech. The words and sounds of Arabic have a richness that evokes great feeling. Arabs love the harmony of word combinations and often concern themselves more with the impact of words than with their meaning. They are inclined to use sonorous words to express themselves. Because of the nature of the language, there is a tendency toward exaggeration, repetition, and the use of metaphors and similes, all of which produce an even stronger effect. The words of an articulate speaker can leave an audience spellbound.

Some Yemenis speak a second language, and English is the most common one. Some older people also speak Russian because of the former connection between the Soviet Union and the PDRY. As a result of migrations, some African languages have reached Yemen.

BODY LANGUAGE

A Yemeni is almost as physically expressive as he is verbally expressive. When talking, Yemenis stand close together and look each other in the eye. It is quite common for members of the same sex to touch each other while talking. A man might clasp another's hand or touch his shoulder. This is the Yemeni way of showing respect and affection.

People also use their heads and hands to communicate. Raising your eyebrows indicates "yes," while blinking both eyes at the same time means "no." To summon someone, you join the fingers of the right hand and then, with the palm facing down, motion toward yourself. To ask a question, you stretch out the thumb and the forefinger at a right angle to each other and curl the rest of the fingers into your palm; then you wave the whole hand back and forth. Even the position of the feet is significant. Yemenis attach great importance to manners, so it is best not to point the soles of your feet at one of them; they consider this act to be extremely insulting.

MEDIA

Yemen's press is among the freest in the Arab world. Despite paper shortages and interference from government officials from time to time, there are still hundreds of newspapers. Many of them are associated with political parties. The English-language *Yemen Times* is well known as a particularly vocal newspaper when it comes to criticizing government policies.

Long ago, people used to greet the imam by kissing the back and palm of his hand and the hem of his robe. Today, kissing the hand is an act of respect to the recipient.

A local man catches up on the daily news at a newsstand in Yemen.

Yemen's mountains are gorgeous, but they obstruct television reception. Despite poor reception, more television transmitters are being installed in mountain villages. Watching television is usually a family activity. In small villages, neighbors and friends often congregate in the few houses with television sets or listen to the radio instead. Yemenis are able to enjoy radio programs from six radio stations.

Yemen has three state-run television channels, plus several repeat channels. Programs are broadcast from Sana'a and Aden. There is now also access to various satellite channels including Yemen Satellite TV. The availability of satellite dishes is spreading fast, bringing Western television shows and news coverage to Yemeni homes. Yemenis enjoy watching soap operas and comedy shows, many of which are filmed in Egypt or Syria. Sporting events are also popular, as are cartoons. The people are also interested in television coverage of their president and government officials. There are a number of locally produced cultural programs and the occasional documentary on Islamic issues or Yemenis overseas.

Internet penetration in Yemen is among the lowest in the Arab region, with approximately 320,000 Yemeni homes having access to the Internet. The two main Internet service providers are TeleYemen and YemenNet, which are operated by the Ministry of Telecommunications. The government of Yemen controls and filters Internet content to its citizens. This is mainly to restrict the access to pornography and some anti-Islamic websites.

Although these intricately crafted daggers come in a huge array of designs, Yemeni men usually further customize their daggers to produce their own masterpiece.

CHAPTER 10

T HERE IS A WEALTH OF CREATIVE talent in Yemen, and artistry is expressed in varied and colorful ways. Visually Yemen is stunning. Fairy-tale—style houses blend with dreamy landscapes. Urban mosques are endowed with exquisite decorations, illustrating the influence of the Islamic faith on artistic expression. The long-standing tradition of poetry reveals the spirit of the Yemenis, and their vivacious nature is depicted in wildly exciting dance and music.

POETRY

The Arab people had very little written tradition before Islam arrived, yet they still managed to develop a rich language of poetry to express their creativity. Instead of writing down a poem, they memorized it and passed it down orally to the next generation. Poetry became a means of preserving a great body of history and tradition.

The Yemenis reserve one of the highest places in their culture for poets, who have played a part in shaping the

A man carries popular books on his head. Poetry is more than just a form of art for most Yemenis; it is also a means of keeping their cultural history alive.

course of events. The powerful words of the poet Mohammed Mahmoud al-Zubayri helped to fuel the republican spirit during the struggle against the royalists. Contemporary poetry blossomed in the 1970s when poets of the new generation, who had not been part of the revolution, began to voice their opinions about the times and their dreams of the future.

Lively, witty poetizing is a popular form of entertainment, and Yemeni poets have perfected the art of spontaneous poetry. A poetry competition is a popular way to show off one's verbal talent and wit. At a wedding, the men from each family will often challenge one other with clever wordplay to entertain the guests. Satirical poetry known as *hija* (HEE-ja) is also a favorite. One poet composes a verse and sends it to a second poet, who responds using the same meter and rhyme.

Tribal disputes are often settled by a genre of poetry called *zamil* (ZA-mil). A tribal poet is the spokesperson for the tribe; his two-line *zamils* are sung by tribal members while they march toward the other tribe. The opposing tribe will then respond with its own *zamil*.

An artist carves Koranic inscriptions on the wall. Calligraphers are masters of patience and concentration. Their art requires a serene atmosphere, removed from the constraints of daily living. Only in such a setting can a calligrapher's inner energy be conveyed to his writing.

There is ample evidence to confirm that Yemenis are masters of "book art." Several ancient manuscripts were discovered in the Great Mosque of Sana'a, some of them from the Koran, others the remains of old documents and amulets. They were delicately calligraphed onto dried sheepskin or goatskin that had been specially prepared for writing. Although paper was known to the Muslims as early as the eighth century A.D., it was not until the 11th century that book production became common. The old manuscript on the right shows Arabic inscriptions on algebra, preserved in the Al-Aqah Library.

CALLIGRAPHY

Calligraphy is a beautiful form of writing, but more important to the Yemenis, it is an artistic expression of Islamic spirituality used to decorate books and mosques.

Calligraphy is not just a case of writing the text; the design should be as full of emotion and ideas as the words themselves. The relation between the black letters and the white space around them produces a striking composition and conveys the true meaning of the written word.

By tradition, the pen used for calligraphy is made from reed or cane. Since calligraphy began when the Koran was first written, the pen is symbolic of the written word of God:

"And your Lord is the most generous,
Who has taught by the pen,
Taught humanity what it did not know."

ARCHITECTURE

There is no doubt that great buildings and temples existed before the arrival of Islam. The province of Ma'rib, once the capital of the ancient kingdom of Saba, is a famous archaeological site. Oral tradition describes a splendid palace called Ghumdan near Sana'a at the beginning of the Christian period, around the time of the kingdoms of Saba and Himyar. According to legend, the 20 stories of the palace towered above their surroundings, and each of the four sides was of colored stone: white, black, green, and red. It was said that bronze lions guarded the entrance to the palace and roared when the winds blew. The alabaster roof was so thin that from indoors one could see birds flying over it.

Historians also confirm that there was an impressive cathedral in Sana'a, built around the same time as the Ghumdan palace. This church, known as al-Qalis, was made of teak and plated with gold and silver.

The arrival of Islam gave a new impetus to building. Just as Christianity inspired the Europeans to build cathedrals, Islam sparked its followers to build places of worship. Mosques were erected wherever there was a settlement. The Great Mosque of Sana'a, which was built in A.D. 630, is a wonder. Much of the material used to build this magnificent mosque was taken from older structures such as the Ghumdan palace and possibly from Sabean temples. Christian decorative motifs such as pigeons, doves, and rosettes appear on the minarets and parts of beams. A remarkable feature of the Great Mosque is its wooden ceiling, which is inlaid with inscriptions and rich decorations.

The minaret of a mosque in Yemen. Notice the exquisite carvings on its outer walls.

THE ART OF HOUSE BUILDING

In Yemen a man's house is his castle. Great pride is taken in building it, and on completion, decorative calligraphic writing records the event on the exterior wall. The house styles in Yemen are unique, and regional variations have evolved over the centuries.

The reed houses in the Tihama villages are round or rectangular with a pointed thatched roof. There is a striking contrast between the simple exterior and the artistic interior. Colorful designs are painted over the entire ceiling, and the inside is decorated with beautifully carved wooden furniture. These reed houses look just like those found across the Red Sea in Africa.

In the coastal town of Hodeida, houses are built in the Red Sea style. These are multistoried, with Turkish windows and balconies, and they reflect the foreign influence on Yemeni building styles.

A house built in the *zabur* style. Because stone is scarce in this arid region, clay is used instead as a building material.

The distinctive *zabur* (ZAH-boor) architecture is common on the plateaus of the eastern and northern highlands. Here there is plenty of clay, but stone is scarce. To build a zabur house, horizontal layers of clay are placed one on top of the other, as though one were making a chocolate layer cake. The walls are then coated with mud. Parapets decorated with small arches adorn the roof edges.

Tall houses are also a favorite in Hadramawt. The town of Shibam is often called the Manhattan of the Desert because it has more than 500 mud-brick skyscrapers, some of which are more than 100 feet (30 m) above street level. Many of the Hadramawt houses are built from mud that has been sun-dried and made into bricks. After the walls have been built, they are plastered smooth with brown earth or light lime plaster.

DECORATION An important part of Yemeni culture is the use of intricate, geometric patterns painted in various color combinations to decorate the houses. The same patterns and motifs that women use to decorate their bodies are painted on walls, windows, doors, and ceilings or carved into plaster and wood. The designs include zigzag lines, dots, floral patterns, and date-palm motifs.

On some houses, the windows are the most decorative element. The *takhrim* (TAHK-rim) windows in Sana'a are well known. They look as though they are covered with lace because their alabaster panes are shaped into delicate patterns. The addition of colored glass makes them even more charming, a wonderful sight to behold.

Doors and windows displaying skilled carpentry work remain as fine examples of the high-quality work of Jewish craftsmen before their exodus. In the south, in cities such as Ta'izz, and in the Tihama, the influence of Indian workmanship can be seen in elaborate door carvings.

This glass window is a typical example of colorfully decorated windows found in the homes of Yemenis.

SILVER JEWELRY

Traditional jewelry made of silver and crafted to local design is popular with women in Yemen. Sometimes colorful coral, amber, agate, glass, or ceramics are combined with the silver to create eye-catching pieces. The markets of Sana'a and Ta'izz are full of glittering head ornaments, necklaces, earrings, bangles, belts, and finger and nose rings. Finely crafted amulets, such as charm cases containing verses of the Koran, became popular after the arrival of Islam.

Yemeni Jews were renowned for their mastery in crafting jewelry. When they emigrated from Yemen in 1949 and 1950, Yemen ran the risk of losing one of its most profitable crafts, so it was decreed that any Jewish silversmith who planned to leave had to impart his skills to the Yemeni jewelers who remained.

Modern lifestyles have altered jewelry habits. Nowadays gold is popular among urbanites, and less traditional jewelry is worn. For a wedding, however, a bride is still always bedecked in the finest traditional jewelry.

Inexpensive jewelry is sold at silver shops like the one above. The quality of some of the pieces compares well with European post-Renaissance jewelry and Ottoman and Indian court jewelry.

DECORATIVE WEAPONS

Weapon making is one of the most valued crafts in Yemen. The distinctive curved dagger known as the *jambiya* is worn on a special belt by Yemeni men. Its design varies according to the region, the tribe, and the social standing of the owner.

The tribesman's dagger is called an *asib* (as-EEB), and it has a bone or wooden handle. It is kept in a leather sheath and secured by a cloth belt. The *asib* is worn in the middle of the body, a sign of a free tribal warrior.

The elite qadis and sayyids wear a dagger known as a *thuma* (THU-ma), which has a slender curve and an ornate silver handle. *Thumas* are kept in embroidered or carved wooden scabbards.

In the past Yemen was renowned throughout the world for making high-quality steel blades. Today many of the blades are imported from Japan or Pakistan.

Making *jambiyas* is a very profitable trade, especially since male Yemenis start wearing them from the age of 14.

The hilt, or handle, determines the value of the *jambiya*, and its carving is a marvel of craftsmanship. The most precious *jambiyas* are those made of African rhinoceros horn, which takes on a rich luster with age. Once carved, the hilts are embellished with silver, and coins are frequently mounted on them.

In earlier times, the *jambiya* was sometimes encased in a silver filigree scabbard. Since this is extremely expensive, most scabbards are now made from special local wood. The craftsman carves two J shapes from wood and then hollows them to fit around the blade. The next step is to bind them together by using strips of goatskin. The dagger in its scabbard is then secured in place with a belt made of leather or finely woven cloth.

DANCING

Yemen has a long-standing and varied dance tradition. Each community has its own unique style of dance. There are dances that are intensely dynamic and those that are more subdued. Some are light and airy, while others involve a lot of hopping about.

One of the liveliest dances is the *bara'* (ba-RAH). Each tribe has its own *bara'*, which is characterized by the number of dancers, the way they command their daggers, the steps, and the music. Only men perform the *bara'*, and always outdoors. It is danced during cooperative work projects, to welcome visitors, on festive occasions and national holidays, or simply when there is enough space to dance and people are in the mood.

Locals perform the traditional *bara'* dance during a gathering in Yemen.

In the northern highlands near Sana'a, as many as 20 men might dance the *bara'* to the beat of drums. Arranged in a horseshoe, the men watch the leader, an accomplished dancer, who stands in the middle and signals a change of step. The men start moving slowly, but the pace soon builds to a feverish tempo, with complicated whirling and intricate steps. Daggers carried in the right hand are used to "cut the air." A great deal of skill is required to coordinate arms and legs so that nobody gets hurt.

Lu'b (li-BAH) is popular in parts of the highlands. The word *lu'b* means "to play," and as the name suggests, this dance is performed solely for entertainment. It is usually accompanied by love songs. A *lu'b* is often danced in pairs, and the partners are good friends or relatives. Sometimes men and women dance together, but only in the privacy of the family home.

MUSIC AND SONG

There is a rich variety of music in Yemen. In the cities, people enjoy the soothing sounds of the oud, a short lute that resembles a guitar. It often accompanies the lovely voices of solo singers. Along the Red Sea coast, musicians use it to play lively rhythms.

Besides the oud, many other instruments are used to produce the stirring sounds of Yemeni music. The *simsimiya* (sim-sim-i-yah), a five-string lyre, is popular in the Tihama, along with cymbals and the violin. There are also reed windpipes, which make high-pitched buzzing sounds, as well as a variety of drums. In the highlands, musicians beat the drums with their hands and often also sing. Ahmad Fathi, born in Hodeida in the 1950s, is a famous Yemeni lute player.

Traditionally woven baskets and pots on sale in a market.

Singing is a popular pastime for Yemenis, and there are many songs for them to choose from: religious songs, poetry chants, romantic ballads. In the past, military songs were very popular, particularly during the revolutionary 1960s. Iskander Thabit from Aden, whose tunes carried many political statements, is practically a legend in Yemen. Today the younger generation enjoys singing modern Arabic-language pop songs.

There are many popular Yemeni singers. One of them is Badwi Zubayr, from Hadramawt. People all over the Arabian Peninsula hum his songs. Famous folksingers and poets include Faisal Alawi, Najib Saeed Thabet, and Shayer al-Khaledi.

CONTEMPORARY TRENDS

In recent years there has been an increased emphasis on preserving Yemen's cultural identity. Cultural centers have been established throughout the country to promote the arts, and tourism has also helped revive some traditional crafts. Traditional poems have been broadcast over the radio and recorded onto cassettes for everyone to enjoy. Two popular folk artists

A CONTEMPORARY PAINTER

Nasser al-Aswadi is one of Yemen's best-known contemporary painters. Born in Ta'izz in 1978, al-Aswadi studied architecture but has worked as a painter for about 13 years. In addition to painting, he teaches art at schools in Yemen.

Al-Aswadi is well known for representing the heritage and traditions of Yemeni culture through contemporary art. Apart from painting, he uses other artistic techniques including engraving and photo transfer. Al-Aswadi is influenced by the interiors of mosques, Arabic calligraphy, and a style of stained-glass windows called qamariyyas *(kah-mah-REE-as). Exhibitions of his work have been held in Yemen and France.*

are the poet Shayf al-Khalidi and the musician Husayn 'Abd al-Nassar. Both come from Yafi, a mountainous region north of Aden, and work together to produce cassettes of poetry. Their work has facilitated a "poetry exchange" throughout Yemen.

The variety of artistic expression is indicative of changing styles in Yemen. Contemporary folk art is thriving. One example is the design and manufacture of metal doors used at the courtyard entrances of houses. The design, colors, and complexity of the work display remarkable talent.

Modern painting has blossomed, and contemporary painters have embarked on a journey of exploration, painting brightly colored landscapes and portraits. The paintings of young artists such as Sabri Abdulkareem, Ali Ghaddaf, Mazher Nizar, and Nasser al-Aswadi are gaining popularity through public exhibitions.

Although most cloth is now imported, cotton and linen are still laboriously spun, dyed, and woven in certain regions of Yemen. The Tihama is known for its striped patterns. Natural dye from the indigo plant is used to create vivid blue and violet colors. In eastern Yemen, some garments are hand-embroidered with delicate patterns.

The bedouin still weave wool from sheep and goats into carpets. Leather goods, such as bags for carrying dates and water, are sometimes still handmade. Along the coast, traditional patterns are woven from palm fronds into baskets, hats, and other useful items.

To promote art, facilities such as museums and galleries are needed. The art movement in Yemen is strongest in Sana'a. There is an art gallery in the capital city, and its National Museum holds exhibitions of contemporary paintings.

LEISURE

Yemeni men relaxing over a card game.

T HE YEMENI WAY OF LIFE involves plenty of social interaction, and the exchange of news and gossip takes place during daily activities such as going to the mosque or the market. Yemenis also spend a lot of time with their families, so much of their entertainment and leisure time revolves around the family.

GAMES

Yemeni children spend most of their time within the family and neighborhood either helping with the household chores or playing with friends. When they do have free time to play, older girls and boys usually have a younger brother or sister at their elbow. Boys tend to be more visible than girls. They are often seen huddling over dominoes or a board game, such as backgammon, in the street or the marketplace. Other popular games include cards and marbles.

Children enjoying games on the television in Yemen.

Girls usually play closer to the home, and their leisure activities are often connected with home concerns and the Yemeni love of poetry. In the afternoon, while their mothers are out visiting neighbors, some girls might play with dolls, while others make up their own games. They might sing, dance, and chant poetry. Sometimes the girls will pick a theme, perhaps beauty or cooking, and hold poetry competitions among themselves.

Some traditional children's games go back to ancient times and have been passed from one generation to the next. Unfortunately few children play these games anymore. Other games and sports such as soccer have replaced them.

SPORTS

A traditional sport in eastern Yemen is camel racing. The governorate of al-Mahrah is known for its well-bred camels that can run very fast because they are slender and extremely flexible. To deter camel thieves, the tribes who breed these prized beasts brand them with various signs. A good camel can cost 150,000 rials ($750).

Soccer is a favorite pastime in Yemen. Children always seem to be kicking a ball around, whether they live in a small village or a city. If soccer balls are

Camel racing was a popular leisure activity in Yemen but has since taken a ceremonial role.

The Honest Person and the Thief

(a traditional game for boys)

Participants: five or more

Equipment: one matchbox (in early days, this game was played with a squared-off bone)

The players sit in a circle and take turns throwing a matchbox into the center. If the matchbox stands on its end, the thrower becomes "king." If it lands on one of the striking surfaces, the thrower becomes either "minister" or "soldier," based on markings made on the box or an agreement beforehand. If the box lands on one of the broad sides, the thrower is declared "honest" or "a thief" (again based on markings made beforehand). The thief receives a "sentence" that is decided by the minister, supervised by the soldier, and agreed to by the king. The sentence might consist of doing sit-ups or performing a service, such as making tea for the other players. Outrageous sentences are discouraged by the fact that any of the players could be the thief in the next game.

O Hillcock, O Hillcock *(a traditional game for girls)*

Participants: any number

Equipment: none

Two lines of girls stand facing each other, stamping their feet to the rhythm of a song. Each team selects a girl who has a talent for spontaneous poetry. A theme is chosen, the first poet comes up with a verse around the theme, and then her team chants her words. The second poet retorts, and the game continues until one of the girls succeeds in silencing the other.

Local men enjoying a game of soccer.

not available, there is always a plastic bottle or a homemade rag ball that will suffice.

Sports are played on a part-time basis. There are very few professional athletes who compete internationally, but there are national league games in the cities. In 1992, Yemen participated as a unified nation for the first time at the Olympic Games in Barcelona, Spain. Yemen has competed in five Olympic Games altogether, but no participant has won a medal yet.

BATHHOUSES

A Yemeni proverb says, "The whole delight of this world lies in the hot bath." Public bathhouses are called hammams, and both men and women use them, although on different days. Bathhouses are an important social activity for both men and women, a place to meet their friends and enjoy each other's company. They are also a favorite place for a bride and a groom to socialize separately with friends and relatives before a wedding.

The bathhouse offers the bathers a place to chat with friends or do a couple of exercises. If it is not too crowded, a group might perform a Yemeni dance while others sing songs.

A typical bathhouse is made up of three interconnecting rooms: the hot room, the warm room, and the cool room. The hot or steam room is normally built with a dome decorated with small glass windows that allow light to filter in. It usually has marble seating areas where the bathers can lie or sit.

Once the bathers have had enough heat in the hot room, they proceed to wash themselves in the warm room. Sometimes they might ask a friend to help them. This is a great act of friendship. Finally they enter the cool room to relax, get dressed, and perhaps rehydrate their bodies by having a refreshing cup of tea. Some may even use the cool room to catch a nap after a massage.

After the bath, the bathers will say to each other, "*Hammam alhana*" (HA-mahm ul-HA-na), which means "A pleasant bath," to which the polite reply is the same Arabic expression.

These men are enjoying a nice, relaxing day at a typical Yemeni bathhouse.

Men chatting and relaxing over some khat.

MEN'S GATHERINGS AND KHAT PARTIES

Chewing khat is an expensive habit. It is possible to tell how well-off a man is by the quality and quantity of the khat he chews.

The afternoons are quiet in many towns because both men and women often attend khat parties, which may last for as long as four hours. The parties take place in the *mafraj* of a house, and everyone takes turns hosting them. The custom is to bring your own khat. Information about where the gathering will take place on a particular day is exchanged in the market or at the mosque.

Since verbal banter and jokes are important parts of Yemen's popular culture, the afternoon parties usually begin with the exchange of good-natured insults and jokes. Afterward weighty subjects such as politics, business, religion, and the economy might be discussed in smaller groups or in pairs. Important business decisions are sometimes made at these gatherings. Quite often poetry is composed and recited. On a special occasion there might be dancing, music, and singing. But there is usually some quiet time at the end of the gathering for enjoying the view or simply for meditation.

WOMEN'S GATHERINGS

Yemeni women are not as restricted as women in many other more conservative countries, such as Saudi Arabia. Even so, most of their activities take place within their home or neighborhood. In the afternoon many women attend neighborhood gatherings. In cities such as Sana'a, women put on their best clothes, makeup, and jewelry to attend what are known as *tafritah* (ta-FREE-tah) circles.

The *tafritah* takes place in the *mafraj* of one of the women's houses. The hostess passes around glasses of sweet tea and bowls of raisins, popcorn, or nuts to nibble on. A few of the women may chew khat. These gatherings offer women a chance to relax, exchange news, and discuss family issues with other women of the neighborhood. They may also listen to music and dance. From time to time, some of the older women will tell stories.

A rare glimpse inside a bedouin women's tent near Sanaw in eastern Yemen.

FESTIVALS

In Sana'a, a tradition has emerged in which the bridegroom and other men drive to the edge of the Wadi Dhahr, a fertile valley of small villages, on a Friday morning to dance. Sometimes several wedding dancing parties go on at the same time.

**Y**EMEN HAS SEVERAL RELIGIOUS and secular holidays that bring its people together at certain times of the year.

RELIGIOUS OCCASIONS

Friday is a day of public prayer and the official rest day when government offices are closed. Every Friday observant Muslim men in Yemen try to offer their midday communal prayers in the mosque, where a religious leader delivers a special sermon.

The prophet Muhammad's birthday is honored by the majority of Yemenis. This is a quiet day that reminds worshipers of their Islamic faith and duties. At home parents might read stories about Muhammad to their children.

Like Muslims in other countries, some Yemenis also celebrate Muhammad's death. On this day, they remember his ascension to heaven. In some areas such as Sana'a, men and children spend the day visiting their female relatives.

RAMADAN AND FASTING

Ramadan is the ninth and most sacred month of the Islamic calendar. On the 29th day of the eighth month, Yemeni Muslims look toward the western horizon for the new moon. If it can be seen, Ramadan begins with the sunset. If not, Ramadan will begin the next day. The month is set aside for fasting to commemorate Allah's revelations to Muhammad.

Muslims fast because Allah has commanded them to do so. Muslims also fast to enrich their spiritual life. A fast heightens spiritual awareness and brings one closer to God. Those who are ill or on a journey during

Local men taking part in a traditional Yemeni dance.

the month of Ramadan do not fast but should later make up for the days lost.

During Ramadan, a drummer wanders through the streets in the early hours of the morning to wake the neighborhood by beating his drum or chanting in a loud voice. Yemenis rise, eat a small meal, and then fast for the rest of the day. The biggest meal of the day is consumed after a cannon sounds at sunset. There is a special diet for this meal, which includes many nutritious foods such as soup, meat or cheese, fresh fruit juices, milk, dates, and figs. Sweets are eaten more than usual to give the body energy and are offered to friends and relatives who visit in the evening. Children often carry a colorful lantern with a candle inside when making their rounds of visits.

In the second half of Ramadan, it is a tradition for children to march around the neighborhood singing songs. They stop at houses to collect nuts, sweets, and donations.

FEASTING

The appearance of the new moon signals the end of Ramadan. At last, fasting is over, and it is time to celebrate Eid al-Fitr, the breaking of the fast. Often abbreviated to Eid, this festival is a time to give thanks to Allah. For many Muslims Eid is also a time to give charity to the poor. It is an official public holiday with no school or work for at least four days.

During Eid, children dress in special clothes bought to be worn only on this day. After breakfast, there are congregational prayers in the mosques, and relatives are visited. Children are then given some money and candies, and everyone eats a hearty lunch.

OFFICIAL SECULAR HOLIDAYS

January 1	*New Year's Day*
May 1	*Labor Day*
May 22	*Day of National Unity*
September 26	*Revolution Day (North)*
October 14	*Revolution Day, also called National Day (South)*
November 30	*Independence Day*

Eid al-Adha, or Feast of the Sacrifice, is another holiday. It starts on the 10th day of the month of the pilgrimage and is the highlight for those who have made the hajj. This holiday commemorates the obedient willingness of Ibrahim (Abraham in the Old Testament) to sacrifice his son to Allah. Many families sacrifice a lamb, which symbolizes giving oneself to God.

SECULAR HOLIDAYS

In spite of unification, Yemenis still observe some of the public holidays observed by the two earlier Yemens. The extent of the celebrations on these holidays depends on the region.

Revolution Day is celebrated in the south on October 14. This commemorates the day that the National Liberation Front (NLF) launched a revolution against British rule in South Yemen.

The final withdrawal of the British and the subsequent formation of an independent state, which later became the PDRY under President Qahtan al-Shabi, is celebrated on November 30 as Independence Day.

Northern Yemenis celebrate their Revolution Day on September 26, the day a group of military officers led by Colonel Abdullah Sallal overthrew the ruling imam in North Yemen and established the YAR.

Labor Day recognizes the contributions of Yemeni workers to the country's economic development. Although the Gregorian calendar's New Year's Day is not a particularly important day for Yemeni Muslims, because of the increasing Western influence, parties are held in some of the larger hotels.

In recent years the official activities and functions that mark the Day of National Unity have taken place at a different city every year. This is to foster a national spirit among Yemenis.

DAY OF NATIONAL UNITY

The most significant modern event in Yemen was the end of national division and the establishment of the Republic of Yemen. For this reason the Day of National Unity, celebrated on May 22, is the most important secular holiday for Yemenis.

In the week preceding the holiday there may be discussions in school about the importance of the day. On the day itself schoolchildren parade through the streets carrying the national flag and singing the national anthem. There are also military parades, traditional dancing and music, and sports events such as camel races and soccer games.

Every year the president makes a stirring speech highlighting Yemen's economic and social progress. The speech is broadcast over television and radio.

Traditional musicians help intensify the festive mood with their lively performance.

In the ancient Middle East, the date palm was a symbol of beauty and victory. The date-palm motif decorated temples, palaces, city gates, and the crowns of kings.

AGRICULTURAL FESTIVALS

Long ago the Yemenis used astronomy as a guide to mark the seasons for planting. One of the most important stars in Yemeni tradition, Sirius, the Dog Star, is the brightest in the sky. In July the dawn rising of this star signals the arrival of the late summer rains that have been, and still are, so important to farmers for irrigation purposes. Planting, harvesting, and the two rain periods remain a time of great rejoicing.

In some regions, ancient traditions are kept alive. Every September, Yemenis and tourists flock to the area of al-Jawf in the al-Mahrah governorate, which borders Oman, to see the fall festival. The event is reminiscent of an ancient festival of that region that celebrated the end of the first monsoon rains.

Farmers share in the bounty of nature by enjoying themselves. During the festival, there is folk dancing and music, as well as sporting events such as camel races and tugs-of-war. Festival celebrations usually conclude with a public banquet.

Considered an important source of food, shelter, and shade—and even, by some, as a source of powerful medicinal and aphrodisiacal power—the date palm was deified by the people of ancient Judea. Since then, many festivals have been held during harvest time in mid-July. In the 14th century the arrival of fresh dates was celebrated with a holiday in the town of Zabid, located in the Tihama. Moroccan scholar Ibn Battuta, who visited Zabid in the 14th century, described the festival: "The people of this city hold the subut al nakhl [feast] in this way—they go out during the season of the coloring and ripening of the dates to the palm groves on every Saturday. Not a soul remains in the town, whether townsfolk or stranger. The musicians go out (to entertain them) and the bazaar folk sell fruit and sweetmeats. The women go out riding on camels in litters."

WEDDINGS

A Muslim wedding in Yemen is a joyful occasion and is often celebrated over a number of days. The marriage ceremony consists of signing a contract in the presence of the qadi, an Islamic scholar of the law, who will recite the first sura of the Koran. The bridegroom's father then throws a handful of raisins on the ground, symbolizing a happy future for the couple. Everyone present tries to gather as many raisins as he or she can.

Women sing and dance around a bride to bring on wedding cheer.

Weddings in Sana'a are usually celebrated in a big way. The butchers arrive early in the morning to prepare meat for the feast. If the family can afford it, several sheep and even a calf will be bought for the meal.

When the groom arrives for the meal, he is accompanied by dancing and singing men. The bride arrives a little later with her father. It is customary for the women of the neighborhood to climb onto the roof of the house, where they welcome the newlyweds with high-pitched singing.

FOOD

A grocery store in Yemen.

T IS A YEMENI CUSTOM TO offer food generously. Guests are treated as royalty, and the host will always say, "Come in and have what there is."

The cuisine is extraordinarily varied in Yemen. Each region has traditional specialties, and every tribe has a distinctive cuisine. Many dishes are made from local ingredients and flavored with numerous spices. Some of the spices were introduced by the ancient caravan trade and came all the way from Indonesia and India.

YEMENI CUISINE

On the whole, the diet is simple and nourishing, making use of locally grown grains such as sorghum, millet, and corn and flour made from legumes. Fruit and vegetables are added to the diet, varying across the country depending on how fertile the land is. Sometimes Yemenis eat chicken and mutton, particularly if there is a special occasion such as the birth of a child, when guests come to dinner, or when a person is ill and is believed to need richer nourishment.

Islam has an influence on food and drink. Muslims do not eat pork or drink alcohol. The Koran advises that pork is unclean.

Men tucking into a typical Yemeni meal of locally produced foods.

The Yemenis are fiercely proud of locally produced foodstuffs, known as baladi *(BAHL-a-di), which means "of the country." Such products are believed to be superior in quality to foreign foods. Yemenis purchase them whenever they are available.*

Locally produced honey is a delicacy that is in great demand. It is an essential ingredient in many traditional recipes. Even a slight variation from the local flavor is an indication that the honey is impure. Honey is also a status symbol and is frequently given as a gift. Some of the most expensive honey in the world comes from the Hadramawt region. Honey also has a medicinal use in Yemen—it is eaten to treat stomach ailments.

THE KITCHEN

Some traditional kitchens in Yemen can be dark because the windows are kept closed to prevent dust from getting into the food. When the cooking fires are lit, the kitchens can become unbearably hot.

Many kitchens in Yemen have at least one *tannur* (TANN-ur), a cylindrical clay oven. *Tannurs* come in all sizes, and women say there is a real knack to breaking in the cook for *tannur* baking. What they mean is that it takes a while to get accustomed to getting the heat of the *tannur* just right so that one can slap the bread onto the insides of the oven. Young girls get lots of practice on smaller *tannurs* before they progress to larger ones.

There is a little hole at the bottom of the *tannur* where bits of fuel, such as charcoal or wood, are put in. When food needs to be grilled or boiled, a grate can be placed over the top opening, and the food placed on it.

Besides the *tannur*, most kitchens are equipped with charcoal braziers to keep coffeepots warm. Many urban homes have gas stoves.

The conventional Yemeni refrigerator is quite an invention. It consists of an alcove in the wall with wooden doors. A big jar of water sits inside. The outside wall has holes, so that when the wind blows through them, evaporation cools the water in the jar and keeps the food fresh. Sometimes when the women are bored, they will peer through the holes to see what is happening in the streets.

For washing up, there is a kitchen sink, which is a shallow trough on a ledge leading to an outside drain. If the kitchen does not have a tap, water will be collected and stored in great earthenware jars.

Cookware is stored on shelves above the oven. There are aluminum saucepans, stone pots, and plenty of breadbaskets. Spices and herbs hang in baskets on the walls. There are rolling pins for dough, pestles for crushing grains, and hand mills to grind corn or pepper. Scissors are used for just about everything—from cutting vegetables to removing the legs from a chicken.

In urban areas kitchens are equipped with all the modern conveniences such as dishwashers and microwaves.

FOOD PREPARATION

In some more traditional families, while the men are out at work, the women get busy with their daily tasks.

Many activities take place in the kitchen. Women often prepare food on trays while kneeling on the floor. To make bread, dough is stretched across a stone and then slapped against the walls of the piping hot *tannur*. While bread is baking, a broth or a stew might be simmering in a clay pot. Meanwhile, with their fingers or a wooden spoon, someone will prepare *hilbah* (HUHL-bah), a dip for bread. *Hilbah* is uncommon in rural areas but is a favorite in the cities. Other popular dips and sauces include tangy tomato, garlic, and red pepper sauces that are mixed by hand or in an electric blender. Bread is dipped into these sauces.

Meat on sale is very fresh, as animals are slaughtered on the spot.

MEAL PATTERNS

For religious Yemenis the day starts early with the dawn prayer. After prayer, some Yemenis have something light, such as tea and a piece of bread. Others wait until 8 A.M. to eat breakfast. This typically consists of scrambled eggs or cooked beans, along with bread or porridge.

Lunch is the biggest meal of the day in Yemen. If male guests are invited, they eat with the men first, and then the women eat. Otherwise the whole family eats together. Lunch in Sana'a might start with a few radishes dipped in a fenugreek sauce to whet the appetite. Then the wheat or sorghum porridge follows, or a cold pancake with a hint of mint or thyme, to satisfy hunger pangs.

A vegetable stew, potatoes, beans, and plenty of bread and *hilbah* ensure that even the heartiest appetite is fully satisfied. Unlike in Western meals, where meat is served during the main course, in Yemen meat is always served at the end of a meal.

For those with a sweet tooth, dessert could be fresh fruit, a caramel pudding, or a hot, flaky pastry with honey. After the meal, tea and coffee are served in another room, where people can relax, and the men can chew khat.

For most people supper is a simple, light meal that the women prepare after the sunset prayer. Supper often consists of the day's leftovers, perhaps chicken or eggs with tomatoes, bread, and water.

TABLE ETIQUETTE

It is a Yemeni custom to share food generously. When offered food, one should accept graciously so that the host is not offended. Refusing food is understood to mean one of three things: The guest feels the host cannot really afford to be so generous; the food is unclean or not prepared properly; the guest does not like the host. Turning down food, therefore, is a social blunder and an insult to the host.

Yemenis eat their meals while sitting on the floor rather than at a table. Before they eat, they have to wash their hands. Yemenis do not use knives, spoons, or plates. Instead everyone eats from communal dishes, taking the food from the part closest to them. Meat and vegetables are scooped up with bits of bread or the right hand.

FAVORITE FOODS AND DRINKS

Every community has its favorite fare. City folk enjoy fruit, honey, vegetable stews, salads, and rice. Along the coast, people eat fish. The tribal people love their local porridges, which are highly nutritious.

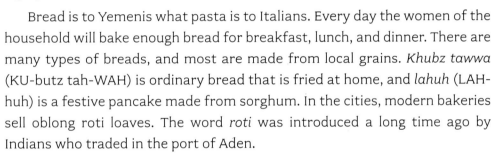

Fried fish, usually sold at the entrance of the fish markets, is a favorite snack among many Yemenis.

Bread is to Yemenis what pasta is to Italians. Every day the women of the household will bake enough bread for breakfast, lunch, and dinner. There are many types of breads, and most are made from local grains. *Khubz tawwa* (KU-butz tah-WAH) is ordinary bread that is fried at home, and *lahuh* (LAH-huh) is a festive pancake made from sorghum. In the cities, modern bakeries sell oblong roti loaves. The word *roti* was introduced a long time ago by Indians who traded in the port of Aden.

The national urban dish is *saltah* (SAHL-tah), which means "soup." The favorites are lamb or thick lentil soup with vegetables such as beans. Sometimes a refreshing green yogurt soup called *shafut* (SHA-fuht), made with sour milk mixed with chili beans and herbs, is poured over bits of bread and eaten in the afternoon.

A typical dessert is *bint al-sahn* (bint al-SA-han), a sweet bread made from eggs. This is dipped in a mixture of butter and honey.

The world-famous Yemeni coffee from the port of Mocha is not as commonly drunk as tea, because it is more expensive. People also drink a flavorful brew known as *qishr* (KU-shir). The drink is made from ground coffee husks and ginger. For those who prefer a stronger coffee, there is *bunn* (BUN), a traditional coffee made straight from the beans. For Yemenis the perfect end to a meal is tea in small glasses, usually very sweet, and sometimes flavored with cardamom or mint.

HALABI KEBAB (YEMENITE MEAT LOAF)

(1 loaf)

2 ½ pounds (1 kg) ground beef

3 tablespoons (45 ml) flour

4 tablespoons (60 ml) oil

1 teaspoon (5 ml) salt

1 teaspoon (5 ml) pepper

1 tablespoon (15 ml) *zhoug* (Yemeni chili paste)

1 cup (250 ml) finely chopped onions

1 cup (250 ml) sliced mushrooms

1 cup (250 ml) chopped parsley

3 eggs

Combine ground beef with flour, 1 tablespoon oil, salt, pepper, and *zhoug*. Form the meat mixture into a 10-inch loaf, making a well in the center for the entire length of the loaf.

Heat the remaining 3 tablespoons of oil in a skillet. Saute together the onions, mushrooms, and parsley until the onions are golden. Place the mixture in the well of the loaf. Lightly beat the eggs and pour over the vegetables.

Preheat oven to 350°F (175°C). Pat the sides of the loaf together to close up the well, and wrap in aluminum foil. Bake for 30 minutes. The loaf may be served either hot or cold.

MALAWACH (FRIED BREAD PANCAKE)

4 cups (500 g) flour

1 ¼ (300 ml) cups water

½ teaspoon (2.5 ml) salt

1 stick margarine

tomato sauce (optional)

sour cream (optional)

Mix flour, water, and salt until dough becomes soft. Add more flour if dough is sticky. Cut dough into two sections. Knead and roll each section into a 20- x 20-inch sheet. Spread margarine on the sheets. Fold each sheet like an envelope with ends meeting at the center. Repeat the folding process to get two layers of folds. Cover with a paper towel, and let it sit for 30 minutes. Cut each sheet into 10 parts. Form each piece of dough to the shape of your frying pan and fry until golden brown on both sides. Serve with tomato sauce or sour cream.

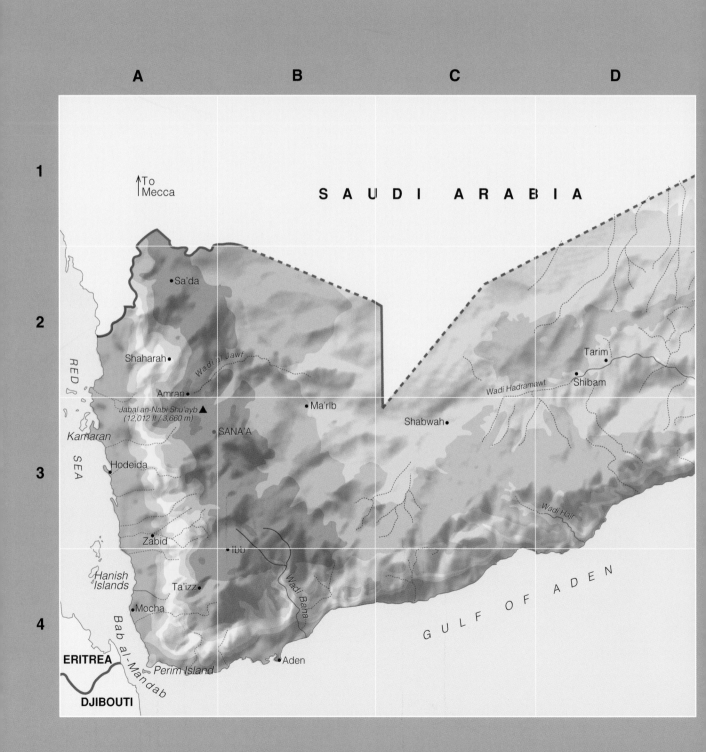

MAP OF YEMEN

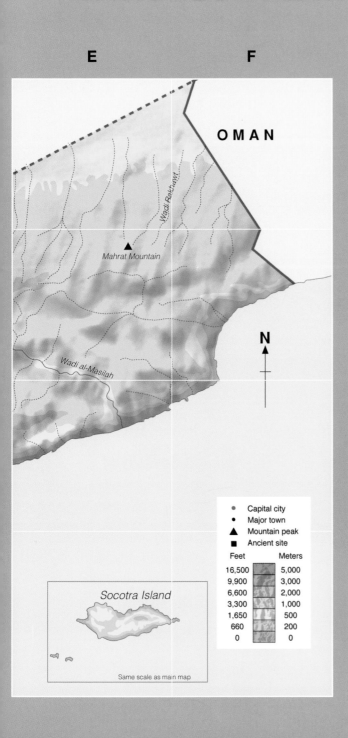

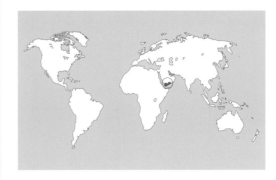

ECONOMIC YEMEN

Services
- Airport
- Port
- Tourism

Agriculture
- Fruits
- Coffee
- Cotton
- Date palm
- Sesame
- Tobacco
- Wheat

Natural Resources
- Gold
- Salt

Manufacturing
- Cement
- Petroleum refinery

ABOUT THE ECONOMY

OVERVIEW

Yemen is one of the poorest countries of the Arabian Peninsula. The discovery of oil boosted the country's sluggish economy, and between 2000 and 2007, the country reported growth of up to 4 percent per year. In 2008, however, growth fell to 3 percent. This was a result of falling oil prices and the global economic slowdown, which directly affected the demand for oil. To strengthen its economy, Yemen has established strategies to diversify its earnings by attracting more foreign investment and supporting its nonoil sectors, including the building of a facility for liquefying natural gas that was scheduled to open in 2009. Approximately $5 billion have been pledged by international donors for crucial development projects. Yemen's economy faces some difficult challenges ahead, as the worldwide financial crisis will more than likely reduce the international aid it currently receives.

GROSS DOMESTIC PRODUCT (GDP)

$27.56 billion (2008 est.)

GDP PER CAPITA

$2,600 (2008 est.)

CURRENCY

Yemeni rial (YR)
$1=199.76 YR (2008 est.)

GROWTH RATE

3.2 percent (2008 est.)

LABOR FORCE

6.494 million (2008 est.)

MAIN EXPORTS

Crude oil, petroleum refining, khat, coffee, vegetables, dried and salted fish, cotton

MAIN IMPORTS

Food and live animals, machinery and equipment, chemicals

TOURISM

404,497 people visited the country in 2008, according to Yemen's Ministry of Tourism, contributing $450 million to the Yemeni economy

MAIN TRADE PARTNERS

China, India, Thailand, Japan, United Arab Emirates, the United States, Saudi Arabia, Kuwait, Germany

AGRICULTURAL PRODUCTS

Grain, fruits, vegetables, pulses, khat, coffee, cotton, dairy products, livestock (sheep, goats, cattle, camels), poultry, fish

NATURAL RESOURCES

Petroleum; fish; rock salt; marble; small deposits of coal, gold, lead, nickel, and copper; fertile soil in the west

CULTURAL YEMEN

Sana'a

Sana'a was declared a UNESCO World Heritage site by the United Nations in 1986. It is a pre-medieval city, fortified by ancient clay walls, containing a host of ancient architectural buildings including mosques, houses, and public baths. A unique feature of the houses in the old city is that many of them resemble intricately decorated skyscrapers—they are flat-roofed towers that are several stories in height. Built more than 700 years ago, Bab al-Yaman, or Yemen Gate, is a legendary entry point through the old city walls. Sana'a is also home to the awe-inspiring al-Jami' al-Kabir, the Great Mosque, which was built in the seventh century and is considered the oldest mosque in the Islamic world.

Suq al-Milh

Suq al-Milh, the Salt Market, is Sana'a's main souk. The best time to visit is in the early morning or the early evening, when it is a hive of activity, bursting with shoppers. There is a wide variety of goods on sale, such as spices, vegetables, corn, khat, pottery, raisins, copper, woodwork, and clothing.

Shibam

Shibam is a 16th-century city surrounded by a fortified wall. Nicknamed the Manhattan of the Desert because of its unique towerlike houses that rise out of the cliff, Shibam was declared an UNESCO World Heritage site in 1982. It is believed that these distinct tower houses were built as a form of protection against bedouin attacks.

Mocha

Mocha is a port city situated on the coast of the Red Sea. During the 15th to 17th centuries, it was well known for being the marketplace for coffee. Merchants from all over Europe came to Mocha to trade. The term mocha coffee is derived from this ancient port. Even today, mocha coffee beans are appreciated the world over for their distinctive flavors. No longer part of a major trade route, Mocha today is dependent on fishing and small-scale tourism. Tourists come to see its impressive landscape along the coast between al-Khokha and al-Makha.

Aden

Aden is a natural harbor that was first used between the fifth and seventh centuries. The port's enviable position on the most important sea route between India and Europe brought it to the attention of many ancient rulers who desired to possess it. Aden has been an urban settlement since ancient times. Legend has it that Cain and Abel founded Aden. Aden remains an important economic and commercial center. Cultural sights include the impressive ancient cisterns, the Tanks; the Palace of the Sultanate of Lahjj; al-Aideroos Mosque; Rimbaud's House, where the French poet once lived; the Tawahi quarter; the Gold Mohur coast; and the colorful market.

Al-Djanad

Al-Djanad is a courtyard mosque located in a tiny village north of Ta'izz. It is believed to be the second mosque built in Yemen, making it one of the oldest mosques in the Muslim world, together with the Great Mosque in Sana'a. It was built in the lifetime of the prophet Muhammad.

Socotra Island

Socotra is a picturesque island situated at the entrance of the Gulf of Aden in the Indian Ocean, approximately 211 miles (340 km) from the Yemeni mainland. The name of the island is believed to have derived from the Sanskrit phrase dvipa sakhadara, or "island of bliss." An island of outstanding natural beauty, Socotra has distinct species of flora including frankincense, myrrh, and Dragon's Blood Tree.

Beit al-Faqih

Beit al-Faqih is located 37 miles (60 km) from al-Hudaydah. It was one of the largest and busiest commercial centers for the coffee trade during the 17th and 18th centuries. It also served as an important storage station for Yemen's coffee crop. The men of this ancient city are well known for wearing unusual short skirts known as al-lahafat. On Fridays the city is host to one of the biggest weekly regional markets in Yemen.

Zabid

Zabid is famous for being the seat of Islamic learning and the site of an important early Islamic seminary. Continuing the tradition, today the city and its surrounding areas are home to more than 80 madrassas, which are dedicated to the teachings of Islam. It was the capital of the Banu Ziyad dynasty in the early ninth century.

Ta'izz

Ta'izz is a city dramatically situated in the highlands close to the famous port of Mocha on the Red Sea. Ta'izz is overlooked by the majestic Jabal Saber. Although it is a modern industrial city, many of its old white mosques and beautiful ancient quarters remain intact. The city is famous for its old citadel and the Governor's Palace, which sits high above the city center.

Wadi Hadramawt

Wadi Hadramawt is the largest wadi in the Arabian Peninsula. The graves of many pre-Islamic prophets and saints can be found there. The Wadi Hadramawt can be entered only through the Rub al-Khali desert and the al-Djol mountain plateau. It is a fertile oasis surrounded by date palms and majestic sandrock mountains. The cities of Shibam, Sayun, and Tarim are located within Wadi Hadramawt.

OFFICIAL NAME
Republic of Yemen (Arabic: al-Yaman)

CAPITAL
Sana'a

POPULATION
23,822,783 people (2009 est.)

MAIN CITIES
Sana'a, Aden, Ta'izz, Hodeida

OFFICIAL LANGUAGE
Arabic

PORTS
Aden, Hodeida, Mocha

ADMINISTRATIVE DIVISIONS
19 governorates: Abyan, Aden, Ad Dali, al-Bayda, al-Hudaydah, al-Jawf, al-Mahrah, al-Mahwit, Amran, Dhamar, Hadramawt, Hajjah, Ibb, Lahij, Ma'rib, Sa'da, Sana'a, Shabwah, Ta'izz

LAND AREA
203,850 square miles (527,970 square km)

NATIONAL FLAG
Three equal horizontal bands of red (top), white, and black; similar to the flag of Syria, which has two green stars in the white band, and of Iraq, which has an Arabic inscription centered in the white band; also similar to the flag of Egypt, which has a heraldic eagle centered in the white band

HIGHEST POINT
Jabal al-Nabi Shu'ayb, 12,336 feet (3,760 m)

NATIONAL EMBLEM
The eagle, a symbol of the strength and liberty of the nation

ETHNIC GROUPS
Predominantly Arab, but also Afro-Arab, South Asian, and European

MAJOR RELIGIONS
Muslim, both Shafi'i (Sunni) and Zaidi (Shia); small numbers of Jews, Christians, and Hindus

BIRTHRATE
42.42 births per 1,000 population (2008 est.)

DEATH RATE
7.83 deaths per 1,000 population (2008 est.)

LIFE EXPECTANCY
63 years (2008 est.)

TIME LINE

IN YEMEN	IN THE WORLD

1500s
Ottomans absorb part of Yemen into their empire but are expelled in the 1600s.

1776
U.S. Declaration of Independence

1789–99
The French Revolution

1839
Aden comes under British rule.

1869
Yemen serves as a major refueling port as the Suez Canal opens.

1914
World War I begins.

1918
Ottoman Empire dissolves as North Yemen gains independence and is ruled by Imam Yahya ibn Mohammed.

1939
World War II begins.

1945
The United States drops atomic bombs on Hiroshima and Nagasaki. World War II ends.

1962
Army officers seize power and set up the Yemen Arab Republic (YAR), sparking civil war between royalists and republicans.

1967
South Yemen is formed; the country is later officially known as the People's Democratic Republic of Yemen (PDRY).

1978
Ali Abdullah Saleh is named president of YAR.

1979
Fresh fighting between YAR and PDRY.

1982
Earthquake kills 3,000.

1986
Thousands die in the south due to political rivalry. PDRY president Ali Nasser Muhammad flees the country and is later sentenced to death for treason. A new government is formed.

1990
Unified Republic of Yemen proclaimed, with Saleh as president.

1993
Coalition government is formed from the ruling parties of the former YAR and PDRY. Saleh declares a state of emergency and dismisses Ali Salim al-Baydh and other southern government members. Al-Baydh declares the independence of the Democratic Republic

1997
Hong Kong is returned to China.

IN YEMEN	IN THE WORLD

of Yemen. Saleh rejects secession as illegal. Northern forces take control of Aden in July. Secessionist leaders flee abroad and are sentenced to death in absentia.

2001

Terrorists crash planes into New York, Washington D.C., and Pennsylvania.

2002

Yemen expels foreign Islamic scholars.

2003

War in Iraq begins.

2005

Resurgence of fighting between government forces and supporters of the slain rebel cleric Hussein al-Houthi.

2006

President Saleh wins another term in the September elections.

2007

Scores are killed or wounded in clashes in between security forces and al-Houthi rebels in the north. Rebel leader Abdul-Malik al-Houthi accepts a cease-fire in June. Citizens are banned from carrying firearms in Sana'a, and demonstrations without a permit are outlawed.

2008

Clashes renew in January between security forces and rebels loyal to Abdul-Malik al-Houthi. In response to a series of bomb attacks on police, diplomatic, foreign business, and tourism targets, the U.S. embassy evacuates all nonessential personnel.

2009

Gunmen open fire at checkpoint outside U.S. embassy in January. The government in February announces the release of 176 al-Qaeda suspects on condition of good behavior. Yemen's parliament approves a two-year postponement of its legislative elections in an attempt to calm tensions between the governing party and the opposition over the fairness of elections. The elections had been scheduled for April 2009 but will now take place in April 2011.

GLOSSARY

abaya
A loose black robe from head to toe; traditionally worn by Muslim women.

bara' (ba-RAH)
Dance with variations in the steps and the number of dancers depending on the tribe.

bedouin
Camel-breeding tribes who roam the deserts.

bunn (BUN)
Traditional strong coffee.

futa (FOO-ta)
Gathered calf-length skirt worn by men.

Hadith
The collection of the prophet Muhammad's sayings that supplements the Koran in guiding Muslims.

hammam
A public bathhouse.

hammam alhana (HA-mahm ul-HA-na)
An Arabic expression meaning "a pleasant bath."

hija (HEE-ja)
Satirical poetry.

hijab
A headscarf worn by Muslim women to conceal the hair and neck; some have a veil to cover the face. Can also refer to the practice of dressing modestly.

h'inna
A Jewish celebration that takes place for the bride-to-be before her wedding.

insha' Allah (EEN-sha Allah)
A social greeting that means "God willing."

khidab (KAY-dab)
Black substance used as cosmetics by women.

lu'b (li-BAH)
A form of dance.

masjid (MAHS-jid)
A place of prayer and worship.

oud
Musical instrument similar to a lute.

qadis
Islamic scholars of law.

saltah (SAHL-tah)
A soup popular in the cities.

sharshaf (SHAHR-shahf)
Loose, black cloak worn by Yemeni women.

sheikh
A tribal leader.

sitara (SEE-tahr-a)
Brightly colored cloak worn by Yemeni women.

tafritah (ta-FREE-tah)
A women's gathering that usually takes place in the afternoon.

tarboosh
A round hat worn by Yemeni men.

tannur (TANN-ur)
A cylindrical earthenware oven.

wadi
A dry riverbed filled in rainy seasons.

zamil (ZA-mil)
A genre of tribal poetry.

FOR FURTHER INFORMATION

BOOKS

Aithie, Charles and Patricia. *Yemen: Jewel of Arabia*. London: Stacey International, 2009.

Damluji, S. S., and Said Bugshan, A. A. *The Architecture of Yemen: From Yafi to Hadramut*. London: Laurence King, 2007.

Dresch, Paul. *A History of Modern Yemen*. Cambridge, England: Cambridge University Press, 2008.

McLaughlin, Daniel. *Yemen (Country Guides)*. Wycombe, England: Bradt Travel Guides, 2007.

Searight, Sarah and Taylor, Jane. *Yemen, Land and People.* London: Pallas Athene Arts, 2004.

FILMS

Bader Ben Hirsi. *A New Day in Old Sana'a*. Felix Films Entertainment, 2005.

Mystery of the Three Kings. Questar, 2003.

MUSIC

Al-Dajamî, H. and Al-Khamîsî, M. *Yemen: The Singing of Sana'a*. Ocora, 2003.

Sana'a Band. *Arabic Folk Dances: Danse Bar'a (Yemen)*, Musical Ark, 2005.

Various Artists. *Yemen: Music from the Heart of Arabia*. Buda, 2002.

Zafa. *Yemen: Funky Grooves of Yemen*. Blue Pie, 2007.

BIBLIOGRAPHY

BOOKS

Hamalainen, Pertti. *Yemen*. London: Lonely Planet Travel Guides, 1999.

Hansen, Eric. *Motoring with Mohammed*. Boston: Houghton Mifflin, 1991.

Johnson-Davies, Denys. *Desert Fox Seif bin Ziyazan*, Cairo: Hoopoe Books, 1996.

Khalidi, Marion. *Queen of Sheba*. London: Hood-Hood Books, 1996.

Mackintosh-Smith, Tim. *Yemen: Travels in Dictionary Land*. London: John Murray, 1997.

Serjeant, R. B. and Ronald Lewcock. *Sana'a: an Arabian Islamic City*. London: Scorpion Communications and Publications, 1983.

WEBSITES

Arab German Consulting, www.arab.de

CIA World Factbook, www.cia.gov/library/publications/the-world-factbook/index.html

Encyclopedia of the Nations, www.nationsencyclopedia.com

Foreign and Commonwealth Office, www.fco.gov.uk

NationMaster, www.nationmaster.com

The UN Refugee Agency, www.unhcr.org

INDEX

INDEX